DON'T QUIT
pivot

Mike Nabors

Published by St. Petersburg Press
St. Petersburg, FL
www.stpetersburgpress.com

Copyright ©2024
All rights reserved. No part of this publication may be reproduced, distributed, or transmitted in any form or by any means, including photocopying, recording or other electronic or mechanical methods, without the prior written permission of the publisher, except in the case of brief quotations embodied in critical reviews and certain other noncommercial uses permitted by copyright law. For permission requests contact St. Petersburg Press at www.stpetersburgpress.com.

Design and composition by Isa Crosta and St. Petersburg Press
Cover design by Isa Crosta

Hardcover ISBN: 978-1-964239-12-5
Print ISBN: 978-1-964239-13-2
eBook ISBN: 978-1-964239-14-9

First Edition

DON'T QUIT
pivot

Never stop loving what you do.
Find other ways to do it!

Do you want happiness at work? Use the skills you've acquired to chase that passion!

DEDICATION

This book is for my heroes: my parents, Joan and Bob Nabors, the ultimate dreamers and passion chasers. Thanks for instilling in me the spirit to follow your dreams and go for what makes you happy.

For my two greatest gifts, my inspirational daughters, Morgan and Ally, please pass this on to your kids one day.

This book is for those of you who feel lost, or as if your life has hit a brick wall. It could be small or big moments that changed the trajectory of your careers. We all go through them. Hopefully, this book motivates you to believe it's never over till you say it is—grab hold of your life!

Contents

Foreword 9

INTRODUCTION
Working For The Weekend? 13

CHAPTER ONE
Do Something That Scares You! 26

CHAPTER TWO
Maximize Relationships 41

CHAPTER THREE
Make Your Trip! 56

CHAPTER FOUR
It's Ok To Quit, But You Better Have A Plan! 64

CHAPTER FIVE
It Only Takes One To Love You,
So Don't Be Afraid To Ask! 84

CHAPTER SIX
Cats Are Cool 92

CHAPTER SEVEN
"Running Errands" 103

CHAPTER EIGHT
Build On Your Foundation 125

CHAPTER NINE
Finding Your Happy "Beginning" 144

Acknowledgments 157
Works Cited 158

Foreword

By Dick Vitale

My life wouldn't be the same if I hadn't taken that leap of faith. If I hadn't pivoted!

My career has been highlighted by two "pivotal" moments. The first happened to me on November 8th, 1979. It was a heartbreaking day, yet an awakening.

I didn't know it then, but that day would eventually give me a new career I couldn't have imagined. That November, I lost something I had worked for my entire life—the dream of coaching basketball.

Being a college coach seemed the pinnacle, but I eclipsed those dreams by making it to the NBA. Yet on November 8th, 1979, the Detroit Pistons fired me, leaving me depressed and hopeless about what would come next.

My rise to the top had been incredible. Seven years after teaching sixth graders, I had made it to the big time, yet I was fired only 12 games into my second season. Basketball has been my passion since I can remember following sports. I loved playing it and was always drawn to coaching.

Yet, just when I thought I had hit a dead end, amazingly, that's when my career pivot took place!

My pivot would be moving from coaching to an unknown, the world of television

Life is funny, as often, it only takes one person to change the course of your future.

Behind the scenes, when I had a successful run as the Head Coach at the University of Detroit, the Executive Producer of NBC Sports, Scotty Connal, was told by his broadcast crew, Hall of Famers Curt Gowdy and John Wooden, that he should write my name down and think about hiring me down the road. They felt that, when I coached, I had the personality, energy, and knowledge to become a successful broadcaster one day. Amazingly, I had a strong recommendation behind the scenes years before my eventual pivot, but it would be a strong connection to my future career. You never know who can help you!

Who would have ever thought that conversation would change my life?

When the Pistons let me go, Connal contacted me quickly. He was no longer at NBC; now, he had been hired as an executive at a brand-new network called ESPN.

When he reached out, I told him I had never heard of ESPN. It sounded like a disease!

I wasn't interested.

I was still longing for coaching and frankly feeling sorry for myself.

My pivot personifies the main tenets of this book, starting with my supportive family and friends.

If you want to stay passionate about your career, you need a valued inner circle who believes in your talents and encourages you to take chances.

My main motivator for making this career-defining pivot was my supportive wife, Lorraine, the leader of my inner circle.

After my firing, she saw me hanging my head for weeks and urged me to try broadcasting. I needed her motivation and honesty to take that leap of faith.

I finally pivoted less than a month after getting fired by the Pistons. You talk about being a rookie again; I had no idea how the television world worked. My first game was in Chicago, calling DePaul vs. Wisconsin. I spent most of the day alone, taking in the Windy City and arriving at the arena hours before game time. My producers were nervous when I arrived, saying I needed to get there much sooner, but this was all new to me!

It's amazing. Once we went on the air, I enjoyed being around the game again and feeling that edge again. It couldn't compare to coaching, but I took to it immediately.

I brought to broadcasting what had made me successful in coaching:

enthusiasm, knowledge, and a needed candidness translated well to my new role at ESPN. When you change your career late in life, you must know that we all have skills to help us pivot. You must apply what you have developed over your career to achieve newfound success. Mike's book repeatedly emphasizes that point.

Still, television and ESPN weren't love at first sight. For the first few years, I applied for college coaching jobs and thought that was where I needed to be.

I didn't trust my pivot!

The turning point came four years after calling my first game, where I worked the legendary 1983 Final Four in Albuquerque, New Mexico.

It was the site of arguably the biggest Cinderella story in college basketball history, where heavy underdog N.C. State upset favorite Houston

Why was this a turning point?

At that Final Four, I saw firsthand the difference I could make as a broadcaster. The upset was great for college basketball, and coupled with ESPN's steady growth, it was fun being part of something that fans were excited about. It showed me the potential I had to grow the game I fell in love with as a young boy.

Leading NC State in that defining season was a young up-and-coming coach named Jim Valvano.

While we became closer when Valvano later joined ESPN, it was amazing how we were kindred spirits. We had a lot in common: We loved college basketball and connecting with people and truly fed off the energy of the fans who enjoyed the sport.

I witnessed Jimmy V's best moment as a coach and, unfortunately, was with him during the worst times of a life taken much too quickly. My friend was diagnosed with terminal metastatic adenocarcinoma, a type of glandular cancer that can spread to the bones, on June 15th, 1992, at the age of 46.

He died from cancer a year later at the age of 47.

Valvano was a fighter to the end, doing everything he could to stay strong for his family and everyone he worked with at ESPN.

The pain he suffered battling this awful disease inspired me to pivot again. I was a few feet away from Jimmy V when he delivered his legendary

"Don't ever give up speech" during the 1993 ESPYS. His words mirrored his actions as he fought cancer as hard as anyone could. His fight motivated me to beat cancer while honoring my friend's name.

I love broadcasting, but my passion to raise money to battle this deadly disease has become my life's work. As I write this, my Dick Vitale Gala has raised nearly 93 million dollars for the V Foundation in our fight to get the ultimate victory: beat pediatric cancer.

Through my pivot from coaching to broadcasting, I learned I could do more than one thing in my life and do it with passion. This mindset has carried over to my continuous goal of raising money for cancer, as this life-changing mission will hopefully save many lives moving forward.

I'll never forget a letter Valvano wrote me shortly before his passing. He advised me to slow down and enjoy my career and family because life is short.

I took his advice, and I firmly believe that if I had stayed in coaching, my stress would have been too much, and it would not have been sustainable.

Pivoting truly saved my life!

Hopefully, this book encourages you to do something I firmly believe in: always follow your passion, but don't be shy about pivoting to newfound happiness and rewarding challenges in your life.

They are there for everyone; you must lean on your inner circle and trust your talents and instincts.

All the best and chase your dreams!

Dick Vitale

Dick Vitale is currently an ESPN college basketball analyst who was inducted into the Naismith Basketball Memorial Hall of Fame in 2008. In addition, he has raised millions of dollars to help fight pediatric cancer. To contribute to Dick's mission, you can log on to: dickvitaleonline.com

INTRODUCTION

WORKING FOR THE WEEKEND?

"Seek a calling. Even if you don't know what that means, seek it. If you're following your calling, the fatigue will be easier to bear. The disappointments will be fuel, the highs will be like nothing you've ever felt."
Phil Knight, Founder of Nike

The motivation for this book comes from everywhere. The words come from friends, family, and peers. They are words of frustration, unhappiness, and complacency from unfulfilled people.

This mindset doesn't discriminate—all ages and every occupation voice it.

I heard it from a teenage worker at Home Depot. "How are you today?" I ask. "Counting down the minutes until I get out of here," he replies.

Ok, he's young. I felt that way working several jobs at that age, but the feeling never disappeared for many.

I ran into someone at another store a few months later. This worker was older but shared the same mindset. "How are you today?" She replied, "Better if I were anywhere but here."

Work unhappiness comes in different layers. Many hate their jobs, but more often than not, we are just putting up with what we do for a living.

When writing this book, I saw a social media post from an old friend which read:

"As I have gotten older and wiser, I discovered that there are six things that I really loved about my job:

Payday, lunchtime, quitting time, vacation time, holidays, and retirement."

Wow...that one blew me away.

Our lives shouldn't be countdowns; we can be happy at the workplace, but it's incumbent on us to find that happiness. It's commonplace for us all to dread Mondays and celebrate Hump Day as if we are so close to being anywhere close to where we work. And then you have one of my biggest pet peeves: TGIF.

"Thank God it's Friday!"

Hey, I love Fridays as much as anyone and understand no matter how much passion we have for our jobs, we all have bad bosses, irritating co-workers and rough days involving our careers, but we spend so much time at work our lives shouldn't be comprised of weekly countdowns to the last day of the workweek.

Wouldn't it be nice to eliminate countdowns and enjoy your job throughout the week? Create the mindset of looking forward to coming to work instead of dreading it!

I encourage my students to drop tired standbys of: "Another Case of the Mondays," "It's Hump Day," and "TGIF" countdowns and attempt to strive for a higher, frankly more enjoyable standard.

How about we ditch TGIF in favor of...

TGIT (Thank God It's Today!)

I know you may think it's corny, but it's a goal we should all work toward. Let's find a career we love so much that we don't celebrate Fridays, Dread Mondays, and raise a toast to Wednesdays as if we're halfway home from a job we can't wait to get away from.

One of my prized possessions is a keychain that one of my students gave me. It reads on one side, "It's not TGIF anymore," and on the other side, "It's TGIT." Priceless!

Looking forward to work and putting in your rearview mirror a job you weren't passionate about should be liberating to all of us.

This book aims to remove this countdown mindset and transform it into one where you look forward to your job, have passion, and feel a greater sense of accomplishment.

I want this book to inspire those who feel empty at work, along with those who found their passion and then, for whatever reason, hit a roadblock that prevented them from reaching places they thought were unreachable for whatever reason.

The first move is rarely easy.

The first step of a marathon, the first brush of a new painting, the first lyric of your first song, or, in my case, typing the first few words to this book. It's all scary, yet at this point, the battle is already half-won. As I type this, I realize I'm officially out of the starting gates.

You can't finish before you start, yet starting shows you can clear an intimidating hurdle.

Often, the toughest part of taking on any challenge in life is overcoming your fears and insecurities and eliminating every possible reason to procrastinate. It all comes down to simply making the first move.

As I type the first few words of this book, it is liberating knowing I overcame a major mental obstacle. When you face any goal, you have to start somewhere, and starting can be challenging.

Consider the numerous doubts we share when trying something new: "I'll never be able to accomplish this," "Why bother? Nobody will care," or, the all too familiar, "I don't think I'm smart enough or strong enough to get through it."

We all create endless reasons why we can't do something. Why it won't work? Why it's not worth the effort, and why would anybody on earth listen to my point of view?

Excuses, insecurities, and, quite frankly, laziness are all culprits that should be replaced by proactiveness, positivity, and, ultimately, productivity. Writing those first few words, taking those first steps, and making those first moves are pivotal to whatever you aim to achieve to get to the ultimate goal.

My specific goal in writing this book is to motivate you to take the first step toward discovering your passion. It's not an easy exercise, but kick-starting the process will lead to a rewarding journey beyond your wildest dreams. This book will give you several examples of those who found their passion early despite overcoming obstacles, along with those who found what they loved the most, only to discover better options later in life. It's never too early or too late to take those first steps.

**The lesson: Never stop loving what you do.
Find other ways to do it!**

It's never easy, but it beats the alternative: ultimately living your life with regrets, knowing you didn't discover your full potential. Many failed to embrace the path best suited for what they love the most. I want this book to enable you to unlock your dreams, knowing it's normal to realize your first move is the toughest. You have to get out of the starting block. You have to start somewhere. That somewhere is better when starting something that will lead to your ultimate happiness.

Taking the first step or, in this case, typing those first few words is the sparkplug we all need to make it happen. Sure, the old cliché, "chase your passion," falls on deaf ears for many, but the goal of this book is to help you not only take the first steps toward achieving your dream but to continue that chase until you reach the finish line.

My goal was to write a book with a purpose that would truly help people of all ages. It didn't matter if you were established in your career or just finding your way. This book aims to help you all. We may share different priorities and problems, but we all crave happiness. Money is great, but is it worth it if you're unhappy?

The foundation of this happiness is our respective careers. Sure, we love our family and friends the most, but work takes up a lot of our time, and it's important to make the most of that time and enjoy it. If we are happy at work, it carries over to the ones we love the most.

This book offers a fresh perspective from those who have made money not because they have chased it but because their passion led them to success. In the same breath, this book taps into those who followed their passion and then pivoted to even greater passions. There are many reasons for the changes, which we can all identify with. Maybe your original dreams didn't work out? Maybe you were laid off and were forced to discover new options? Or maybe you just lost your love for your initial passion? That doesn't mean you must quit doing what you like—it's time to pivot!

A key tenet in this book is we all have dreams, yet we all have skills and talents. The goal is to motivate you to do what you have been waiting for. Don't wait, and don't quit because your original dreams didn't work out as you planned. Do it now! The longer you wait, the more excuses you can make on why change isn't realistic or practical, It's all realistic and practical. You have to put a plan in place!

You may not know what that is. But this book's purpose is to guide you in that direction! As my late and great father repeatedly told me (especially during the low points in my life), "You only get one at-bat, Buddy." Think about it. What is your purpose? Why wake up every day dreading what you do? Wouldn't it be refreshing to go to bed looking forward to the next day? It's important to have something to look forward to in this life. Let's change your mindset and give you the happiness you deserve. This is the core message I want to pass on to you from both my experiences and the respective journeys of those who have found success by following their heart and pivoting to something they love even more.

As a college professor, I stress to my students the importance of finding happiness in whatever they do moving forward. To emphasize the point, on the first day of every new semester, I greet them by playing this song by the legendary eighties rock band Loverboy:

Everybody's workin' for the weekend
Everybody wants a new romance
Everybody's goin' off the deep end
Everybody needs a second chance

The message is that I hope my students, or anyone else, never have a job where they are "Working for the Weekend." You should enjoy the week, too! Sadly, yet consistently, studies show that most people count down the days till the weekend because they either hate their jobs or have no passion for their work.

This book will encourage you to change this mindset!

You must treat your work relationship like the other important relationships in life, with respect and love. Passion is everything, even when it involves your career. The bottom line is that if you love what you do, it feels less and less like a job, and you'll get more out of it.

Get more out of your life!

I was surprised when I read a paper from one of my students who declared after reading a book that prioritized working in a job you love that it was the first time in her life that she realized she could like her job. This belief stemmed from her parents, who hated the jobs they worked their entire life. The concept of being passionate about a career was something new to her. Her mindset, I have found, isn't an isolated case. Many of us feel we have a certain career because others want it for us. A common mindset regarding our occupational choice is finding a more stable job. Often, we choose a career because we feel that's what our family and friends want for us—but what do we want for ourselves?

You should do what makes "you" happy. It's your life—a happy career is vital to the quality of "your" life.

We all have goals. Some we attain quickly; others take time to achieve. Still, others feel impossible to reach, and we think, 'I want to do it, but I never will.' For me, that was writing a book. For years, I had the passion but didn't have the purpose. Furthermore, I didn't have the gumption to take the plunge.

I talked about writing a book to so many for so many years. I got tired of hearing myself yapping about it to the point where I wasn't sure what I would write about, yet it seemed to have the perfect title: "Shut up and write the damn book!" Stop talking about the message, hotshot, and make it happen!

Many of us, deep down, think we can do things we are passionate about but don't follow our dreams. In other instances, we follow our dreams but let them die when they die. We don't pivot our respective passions to even greater heights.

That's what this book is all about! Stop talking and start doing! You only get one at-bat in life. Make the most of your chances and do something you enjoy.

While I was growing up, my father repeatedly told me that when I was older, sitting on the front porch (ok, it's a metaphor; even if you don't have a porch and/or a rocking chair, stay with me), the thing you will pass on to your grandchildren isn't all the money you earned or the materialistic possessions you acquired, it's the worthwhile accomplishments you are most proud of. Specifically, your life experiences: the chances you took, the fun you had, and the feats you could master when you pushed yourself the hardest.

It could be starting the business you've spent years talking about, climbing Mount Everest, running a marathon, or, for some of us, sitting down and hammering out that book you've long talked about.

Many of us have "that thing" we have been putting off! Don't live your life without doing "your thing."

Honestly, taking the first step is the hardest part. As I write this, I feel good knowing I am crossing that hurdle for this project. Getting out of the starting gates is tough, but the momentum you build is the ultimate motivator to push you forward in whatever you set out to do.

FOLLOWING YOUR PASSION

We all possess a talent or a unique quality. It took me a while to figure out what mine was. I was never a gifted student or athlete. I never recognized any special skill. My unique advantage: I always knew what I wanted to do.

I'm unsure of the exact moment, but I would guess it would be around fourth or fifth grade. That's when I realized I would not be a pro athlete. The self-awareness of my athletic limitations, complemented by the lightbulb that came on in my brain when I discovered it was possible to get paid to cover sports, was a tipping point for me. It was an amazing awakening where I thought, "Let's get this straight—you can go to games, watch them for free, and they pay you for this?"

I knew at a young age I wanted to be a sportscaster.

My dream wasn't a focused plan, more of an abstract goal, but it would happen come hell or high water. I talked about it with my friends in middle school. I furthered the conversation in high school, where I remember a classmate wishing me the best in my endeavor, writing in the yearbook my senior year that he wanted me to become "Howard Co-Nabors" one day. This was, of course, a tribute to the late and great famed broadcaster Howard Cosell.

When I wrote my first book on my collection of interviews with future Hall of Fame quarterback Drew Brees, it was gratifying to have so many old classmates reach out and remind me of how I used to talk about being a sports journalist. It felt good to know I had acted on my passion. It felt better knowing I had routinely pivoted within my passion for years.

The profession wasn't always good for me. I was laid off after the birth of not one but both of my daughters. The lesson for me is you must love something so much even when it doesn't love you back.

Then, I discovered the most valuable lesson: Don't give up on what you enjoy when your passion hits a roadblock. Use your love of the craft and acquired skillsets to pivot towards a new passion. It's something I have repeatedly done in my career. After doing this successfully over many years, a set of experiences motivated me to write this book to help those facing similar situations. Pivoting within my passion continued my goal of always enjoying what I do for a living. It doesn't matter if you are a middle-aged sportscaster, a lawyer, a doctor, or an accountant. It's never too late to try something else or build off the skills you have spent years and sometimes decades accumulating.

My purpose is to inspire others not to give up on their dreams but to pivot toward the goals they have been discussing for years. You have to take action!

I have admired successful people my whole life, not because they made a lot of money but because they pursued their passion no matter the obstacles. They had a dream, chased it, and savored the rewards of achieving their goal. Some athletes don't like sports. They like the money they make from sports. Some doctors and lawyers don't like treating patients or arguing cases. They like the paychecks that come with those jobs.

But for many, it's not about the money. It's about the craft. Practicing that craft is the reward they reap at the end of each day. When they kick back in those metaphoric rocking chairs and talk to their grandkids, their joy stems from the fact that they followed their passion and inspired others to do the same. We all have a reason for endless joy, and it's up to us to pursue it.

This book will present my best examples of those who have found the summit of financial success only because they love what they do. In all of these examples, I firmly believe they would have loved their work even if they had not made millions doing it.

My case studies include famed musician, singer, and songwriter Dave Grohl. Tony Hawk is the ultimate outlier and the most famous skateboarder ever. And comedian Jerry Seinfeld, who could have ridden off into the sunset after making millions of dollars with his legendary TV show but still practices stand-up comedy. Why? Because he loves it. That love is at the core of each of these examples. It's why they do what they do, and that passion overrides their material motivations.

Along with providing those success stories, I have complemented this book with my theme of pivoting from your passion. For these purposes, I incorporated perspectives from those I have seen achieve success in this way. What do all of these examples have in common? They all grew up wanting to be sportscasters but have pivoted to five careers in recent years and achieved great success.

These five examples have gone from covering sports to the following: becoming a financial analyst, a trainer, a real estate agent, a CEO of his self-made auctioning company servicing organizations all over the country to someone who spent decades as a broadcaster and is now successful as an entrepreneur selling a famous family recipe. These are real-life examples of five people who did the same occupation for years but at different stages now enjoy life in ways they previously could have never imagined.

Don't quit ... pivot!

In this book, I provide instances of those who have bravely jumped from what they love to what they love as much, if not more. Sprinkled in are the backgrounds of Grohl, Hawk, Seinfeld, and others who have reached the pinnacle of success but would be just as happy without all the fortune and fame because their passion provides enough fulfillment.

This project canvasses the mindset of those who have found success, but you will travel down many avenues in this book. The examples from those who have pivoted towards new horizons are wrapped up in nine chapters. Those chapters encompass keys to finding happiness by pivoting to your passion.

Before we get to the meat of this sandwich, let me deliver an appetizer, an example of one of the most inspirational athletes I ever encountered during my many years as a sportscaster. He may not have a household name, but he is an inspiration to me and a tried-and-true example of growing in your life by using all the skills you have accumulated for years to find a new realm of contentment.

Randall Gay was a huge success in his football life, but the admirable part is he would have been fine without football. Growing up in Baton Rouge, Louisiana, he was a gifted straight-A student. He was also a great all-around athlete who excelled in track, weightlifting, and football. Despite only playing eight games his senior year of high school, Gay rushed for over a thousand yards and accounted for 18 touchdowns.

Randall stood out so much as a football player that he earned a scholarship to Louisiana State University, where he was a starting defensive back on the school's first National Championship team in forty-five years. Gay waited for his name in the NFL Draft, but it never was called.

And that is where things pivoted in a remarkable winning fashion. A winning trend that proved historical.

Undrafted but undeterred, Gay went from the National Champion LSU Tigers to the defending Super Bowl champion New England Patriots. Much like Tom Brady, a once-upon-a-time draft-day afterthought, Randall Gay quickly rose to earn a starting spot at the next level.

Once he wore an NFL helmet, Gay showed he could climb the ladder to success and made the most of his newfound opportunities. In his first NFL training camp, Gay beat out Christian Morton, the Patriots' 7th-round draft pick, to make the team. Later in that same season, he jumped into the starting lineup due to injuries to veterans Ty Law and Tyrone Poole and went on to start for the Patriots in their victory in Super Bowl XXXIX.

Two years later, Gay was part of the Patriots team that became the first in the NFL to post a perfect regular season since the Miami Dolphins accomplished the feat in 1972. However, those Patriots fell short against the Giants in a Super Bowl XLII loss. For Gay, though, that's where the story gets even better.

As a free agent the following spring, Gay signed a contract with the New Orleans Saints, and in his second year with the Saints, he became a big contributor to the first Super Bowl win in New Orleans franchise history. So, if you're counting, across seven years, Gay played a significant role on three championship football teams, including two that played in his home state.

But Gay knew he would pivot from his passion throughout this remarkable football journey.

A year after winning that Super Bowl with the Saints, Gay approached New Orleans Head Coach Sean Payton during the team's mandatory offseason workouts to ask about getting an excused absence so he could take his law school entrance exams. Gay wasn't nervous about confronting Payton because he was prepared to put forth a good case. "I knew I might have to argue a bit," Randall said. "We had just won a Super Bowl, and everybody was talking about a Super Bowl hangover, and these practices are mandatory, and I'm asking to be excused for something that wasn't related to football or the team in any way?"

The Saints' Head Coach let him slide and, to Payton's credit, saw the benefit in Gay's unique audible. "It was more like he expected me to do it," Gay recalls. "He expected that from his players. He said, 'Those are the players I want on my team.'"

Randall would retire in 2011, and in the coming years, instead of resting on his NFL laurels and the millions he made, Gay would pursue his next passion. Finally, in 2015, he and his wife graduated from law school and immediately started practicing. Gay is now a successful juvenile prosecutor and assistant district attorney.

Pivoting from the NFL to the private sector as an attorney, Gay thrives in his current passion and sees similarities with his old one. "It's a competition, and you are competing," he said. "It's one side against another side. If I'm not going to be doing that in football, I can do it at least in something else."

Gay's example personifies the motivation for this book. Just because you have a passion for one thing doesn't preclude you from jumping to a new arena you will love just as much, if not more.

Another major theme I pass on is when you decide to pivot. You can use the foundation of skills you've acquired to make that move. This doesn't have an age limit. In the coming chapters, you will learn about those who pivoted in their 30s, 40s, 50s (me), 60s and beyond.

Gay is the perfect example of someone finding a new career using the skills and attributes he accumulated in his initial passion. Playing in such a regimented profession helped him in his second life as an attorney.

"It parallels so much with the discipline part," he said. "Football got in my head that I would not be late. Often, for court in the morning, I'm the first one in there. I beat the bailiffs. I beat everyone. I'm just sitting there waiting."

For Gay, punctuality and sticking to the routine helped him transition from football to practicing law, and so did playing in the spotlight, covering the world's biggest and fastest wide receivers for years in the NFL, which assisted him when he transitioned into his academic endeavors.

"Even in law school, when people were nervous about things, I was like, 'Dude, this is not pressure, trust me,'" Gay said with a chuckle.

The stress he endured weekly as a pro football player helped him adjust to the pressures of becoming a lawyer. "It makes me (think to myself), 'You know how to do this. You've been dealing with tough situations like this your whole life. Just go with it.'"

Throughout the process, Gay appreciated his journey, where all the hard work re-emphasized his belief that pivoting from football player to attorney disproved many misconceptions about the ability of athletes to make such a move. "I do take it personally when people think that football players are dumb," Gay said, "because, over the years, athletes have proven to be some of the smartest people on this earth because the stuff you have to learn to play football to reach the NFL is crazy."

Gay would know. He made a rare pivot from the NFL to the courtroom, but his example represents the heart and soul of this book. Having one dream doesn't preclude you from following another. When you make the pivot, you aren't empty-handed. It doesn't matter what your first career is. You could be a lawyer, doctor, engineer, hair stylist, sportscaster, or former NFL player. We all have skills. It's up to us to figure out how to best use them to create newfound happiness.

Often in life, we take things for granted, ourselves included. We all have unique skills, experiences, and traits, and they can all create unique opportunities.

This book's mission is to help you realize all the possibilities!

CHAPTER ONE

DO SOMETHING THAT SCARES YOU!

"Courage is resistance to fear, mastery of fear-not, absence of fear."
Mark Twain

Darius Rucker is a three-time Grammy award-winning singer and songwriter. He's the proud owner of 10 number-one hits, but amazingly, after performing in front of packed arenas for decades, he still can't shake one constant.

"I get nervous every night," Rucker told sports host Dan Patrick in a 2022 interview. "I think if I stop getting a little nervous, I'll stop playing."

Like many top performers, Rucker feeds off of the nerves that keep his performances at a high level, maintains the hunger for his craft, and keeps him honest that he can't rest on his laurels. "Are you nervous you're going to forget words?" Patrick asked Rucker. "No more nervous you're gonna miss notes. I'm 56 now. I got a teleprompter, and I'm not so worried about the words. It's more about hitting bad notes more than anything else."

Hearing the words of one of the most successful musicians in American history talk about being scared to perform should be a lesson to us all.

Everyone gets nervous. They just show it in different ways. Being nervous, means you care!

For all of us, the pandemic was a game-changer. It gave us time—LOTS of time—to think and reevaluate, and for some, it motivated us to change how we approached life before vaccines, masks, and remote workspaces.

For me, it served as the ultimate motivation. I didn't know how to handle the thought of being secluded in my home, unable to go to the gym or a restaurant, and being denied the opportunities to advance my career objectives while growing my production company.

Like many of you, I couldn't afford to sit back and wait for the madness to end. My company was my livelihood. Its success depended on me taking the initiative and creating new options. I approached it as the classic case of turning a negative into a positive. Now is the time to do many things you have considered for years.

It was time to make it happen.

The procrastination accumulated for years and involved many areas I had considered pursuing, including teaching, writing, and speaking. With newfound idle time over the pandemic, I finished my master's degree, which opened the door to teaching opportunities. To graduate, I had to write a thesis; it was the perfect prerequisite for writing my first book. In one year, I pivoted from being a sportscaster and business owner to new options, including being hired as a college professor and publishing my first book.

It was the classic case of pivoting to new passions. I always wanted to be a sportscaster but discovered I had much more to offer.

We all have more to offer!

Remember that you can often create new options while keeping what you have. For example, sportscasting will always be a part of my work. I just wanted to evolve and accomplish more goals while creating more stability and, frankly, more freedom. Adding to my plate, I accomplished all of the above.

Making these changes is tough, especially after you've done something for years and decades. You get comfortable and feel the career you're in is all you can do. But we can always do more than we think.

Don't take yourself for granted!

DO SOMETHING YOU'RE SCARED OF!

The first step in pivoting is doing something you're scared of. What does this mean? It's pushing yourself to new heights you may have thought about but weren't sure you could conquer. Doubting your ability to make such life-altering moves is a normal emotion, yet the secret to overcoming your fears comes down to taking that initial plunge.

Fight your fears!

We often hear age is just a number, and it is, but some numbers mean more to others. I didn't think twice about turning 30 or 40. For some reason, turning 50 hit me hard. It was the ultimate wake-up call. Suddenly, I needed to do everything I had talked about for years. I thought, 'If you don't do it now, it will never happen, and you will forever regret it.'

Need a little motivation? Consider this: you're retired and playing with your grandchildren, telling them about your life—all but that part where you didn't chase all the dreams you could have. I never wanted to have that talk with my grandchildren. Turning 50 pushed me to turn things around so that one day, I would pass on to my grandkids how I took a stand in the middle of my life and changed it all—and during a global pandemic, no less!

Doing something you're scared of doesn't have an age limit or an experience level. Actress Jennifer Grey is known for her lead role in the popular movie "Dirty Dancing," but decades later, she was scared to make a comeback doing, of all things, dancing. Grey told Parade Magazine that conquering her fears on the TV show "Dancing with the Stars" was beneficial. "I realized it was just fear of being embarrassed, fear of the humiliation. I decided that the only way to deal with anxiety is through exposure. So, I said, 'I'm going for the thing that I'm afraid of because on the other side of that is freedom.'"

One of the most impressive "pivoters" is Pro Football Hall of Famer Michael Strahan. He has done so much since he left the game that most of this generation know only of his TV career. It's hard to imagine a former athlete who has pivoted from his passion more than Strahan, whose broadcasting trek began, like many former players, as a football studio analyst with FOX Sports. He still holds that job, but the remarkable part of Strahan's pivot is his astounding success in his new role. Since leaving his football playing career, Strahan has won a pair of Daytime Emmy Awards for his work as a co-host on Live! with Kelly (Ripa). In addition, he has hosted a game show (Pyramid) and pivoted again by co-hosting Good Morning America (GMA).

Moving from sports to GMA was far from easy for this one-time intimidator of quarterbacks because he found himself scared straight on television. "At FOX, I don't get nervous anymore; Pyramid, I don't get nervous; GMA, I get nervous," he said on Rich Eisen's podcast, "Just Getting Started, Voices of the NFL."

"The payoff to me has been the fact of being able to do something that I never thought I could do, that a lot of other people never thought I could do," Strahan added. For this former player, it wasn't about the money. It was about the challenge. But the new jobs didn't come without overcoming his fear of failing.

After becoming a successful NFL studio analyst with FOX, a turning point in Strahan's career came when he found himself in unfamiliar territory, co-hosting the Academy Awards red carpet preview. It's a feeling looking back, he told Eisen, he will never forget.

"I am scared to death," he said. "This is Hollywood, this is big stars, a black-tie affair, the Oscars, man. I watched that; I'm not supposed to be on that red carpet. I was scared (out of my mind)."

For one of the most intimidating football players of all time, feeling vulnerable was a foreign emotion. But an assist from a peer, former sportscaster and Good Morning America host Robin Roberts, changed everything. "I see Robin across the way and go over to see her," Strahan said. "She looked at me and said, 'How are you feeling?' I said, 'Robin,

I'm scared.' She goes, 'Hey, you got this, don't worry. I came from sports too, you belong here.'"

At that moment, Strahan felt the exchange delivered him both the confidence and sigh of relief he needed. "It completely changed my life," he said. "With that one little thing, I saw Robin Roberts and knowing that she came where I came from (and) how I didn't even recognize that because she is so great at what she does now. (For her to say) 'You belong here' meant the world to me."

Those words of encouragement helped catapult Strahan into one of the most transformational media voices of our time and helped him succeed as one of the ultimate pivoters. His career is another example of how being scared is okay, that taking chances and pushing yourself can take you to heights you never expected to reach.

The lesson: Doing something that scares you gives you the confidence to advance and excel in whatever passion you pursue.

It's liberating to do something you're scared of. I remember getting my first big break as the host of the NHL's Tampa Bay Lightning pre- and post-game television broadcasts. After years of grinding it hard in local news at small, medium, and large markets, this was the opportunity I had clamored for.

There was just one problem. In all my life, I had seen just "one" hockey game live. I had grown up watching football and baseball and was far more knowledgeable about those sports than hockey. Yet, there I was, stepping into my dream job as the host of several 30-minute shows per week.

Scared? You bet I was scared. Terrified might be a better word to describe it. But that fear of failure proved to be the ultimate motivator. It forced me to work harder, and when I succeeded, I reveled in the fact that overcoming my fear helped fuel my success.

It's OK to be scared!

Being scared and overcoming your fears is essential to pivoting toward success. Escaping from your comfort zone and finding comfort elsewhere gives you a unique sense of empowerment that can be used as fuel to help you clear other hurdles. It's easy to stay in the right-hand lane your whole life, but taking hold of your dreams, pivoting to the left lane, and forging ahead will take you places you never thought you could go.

Ten years after hosting my first Lightning game, I reached the first true crossroad in my career. I was starting to see my business change. Local news jobs didn't pay like they used to, the newspaper industry was dying, and regional and national sports networks were laying off extremely talented people. I had to accept that I couldn't rely on just being a sportscaster anymore. I had to create more options in my life to support my family.

But I didn't want to sacrifice doing what I loved!

I decided to start my own company, which produced documentaries, and continued hosting shows for sports networks, but that all changed when I met a woman on a flight from New Orleans to Tampa. She was the Vice President of a nonprofit organization that assisted various kids in need. She told me she was looking for a prominent figure to front a public service announcement (PSA), someone who could identify with her organization and deliver a message that backed up their mantra of hope and redemption. I immediately thought of an NFL player who could be perfect as he had overcome a troubled childhood and a drug addiction to win a Super Bowl just the previous year. I later brought the player to the nonprofit, and it was a successful shoot.

It was also a turning point in my life.

At that moment, I suddenly realized for the first time that I could be more than just a sportscaster. The lesson is that we can all be more than we are now, more than what our initial passions lead us to become. But we often have to jump out of our comfort zones to make that happen. And that's scary. But it can be oh-so rewarding!

Since finding a frontman for that PSA, my company has represented Fortune 500 companies, a wide variety of businesses nationwide, and a myriad of nonprofits. That PSA gave me newfound confidence that I could tackle any subject matter.

I'll never forget going into a meeting trying to help a local government entity find a viable way of producing videos that would help the county's growing problem of curbing addiction to prescription drugs. I never could have imagined myself being in a meeting like this a few years prior, but it became natural because of my background. I had a passion for building relationships as a sportscaster and carried that passion into my efforts as a newfound entrepreneur. In addition, my years as a broadcast journalist enabled me to consume many different subjects and quickly turn them into stories daily. This skill set helped me as a business owner. We all have skills we take for granted. It's our responsibility to use these skills to take our respective careers to heights we couldn't have previously imagined. The possibilities are endless.

Push the boundaries of your passion!

I was scared in my 30s to bring my sportscasting abilities to a network stage. I was scared in my 40s to pivot my passion for forming a successful business, and here I was in my 50s, overcoming more fears. My previous experiences helped me during the pandemic to create options and become a successful college professor, author, and speaker—in less than a year!

It was scary but so worth it!

Authors Dorie Clark and Natalie Nixon wrote an article in the Harvard Business Review titled "The Challenge of Leaving a Long-term Job to Start Something New." The article touched on the fear of changing an occupation that has been your foundation for years and provided six specific challenges for fighting the fear of pivoting toward greener pastures at the workplace.

This article was based on both authors' experiences. Nixon pivoted from a 16-year career in academia to a role as an independent consultant. Clark drew her research on the many clients she coached during her long career as a consultant, author, and current professor at the Columbia Business School.

According to Clark and Nixon, the six challenges of pivoting involve:
- **Ruminating and Second-Guessing:** It's human nature to wonder if you're making the right move, but Clark and Nixon recommend you ask yourself simple questions such as, "Would I enjoy my new challenge?" and "Could I make money?"

- **Feeling Guilty**: You may not like your job, but will you feel guilty leaving a work family that you do like? Often, we have to separate great co-workers from a greater opportunity in our next career.
- **Being afraid of losing status:** Clark and Nixon touch on reality for many: We may not be happy in our careers, but we possess great recognition, responsibility, and respect in a job. Can we leave all of that behind for happiness?
- **Needing to Adapt:** The older we get, the harder it is for many to change their ways and adapt to new workplace rules. We may not like our current jobs, but we are creatures of habit and have gotten used to routines. Can we evolve and adapt to our new career, which promises more substance?
- **Managing the Perception of your new colleagues:** You may love your new career but have difficulty relating to your new co-workers who routinely preach, "This is how it's been done around here for years." Can you play well with others? Finding happiness may take lots of deep breaths and patience.
- **Balancing Opposing Emotions**: Clark and Nixon bring up a great dilemma facing many bold enough to make a career move later in life. It's often a balancing act between being 50 % terrified and 50% exhilarated.

These challenges align and are common obstacles for many who crave change. "The way I would sum up the challenges is when someone is making a professional change after a long career, it can evoke a lot of challenging emotions, especially related to your status, in your place in the world, and because of that, we need to be aware that might happen so you're not blindsided by it. You need to be aware of it so you can deal with it head-on," Clark told me.

Dorie Clark has written for years on the art of starting over in the workplace. She is the Wall Street Journal bestselling author of "Reinventing You," "The Long Game," "Entrepreneurial You," and "Stand Out," which Inc. magazine named the #1 Leadership Book of the Year.

She has witnessed how fear itself is the biggest fear for many in pivoting. "Fear can definitely hold people back when they are changing careers," Clark said. For many, she concurs that the scariest aspect is taking a step backward in your new endeavor.

"In the beginning, you're not going to be as good as you were at the thing you are leaving," Clark said. "That can be a little demoralizing to one's self-esteem. You might actually have to take a step back temporarily in terms of your title or your status because you need to regain ground in your new field. It can force a lot of adjustments both to your paycheck and your identity."

Pivoting isn't easy, but the rewards can be life-changing. The newfound freedom and happiness and the absence of stress from your previous job give your life a new purpose.

You must trust your instincts.

Clark's book "Reinventing You," touches on the stress we often put on ourselves when fighting the fear of change. Clark tells me, "We logically as humans want to preserve our status in the eyes of other people. So if we embark upon something new and it actually turns out we're not that good at it, or we decide we don't like it, that threatens to make us look not as competent, not as decisive as we might like to project to the rest of the world. Because there's that risk, it engenders fear in some people."

"It's not that it's so much harder to change careers when you're 50 or 60 compared to when you are 23, but the issue is more what you have to lose. It's a question of loss eversion. When you are 23, and you've only been in a job for a year or two, you actually haven't built up that much salary. You haven't built up that much status. You're going from one thing to another, but sort of who cares."

Let's face it: pivoting isn't for everyone. Some are content with their career path, while others look forward to a life of retirement without work. Still, for many, the search for their passion consumes them, whereas fighting the fear and having the gumption to move forward gives you the confidence to test your boundaries.

Overcoming your fear, making that pivotal move, and offsetting the sacrifices needed often equates to a better life with a career that makes you the happiest you've ever been.

Doing something you're scared of gives you a new life.

"It's a nice reminder that we're not just tailor-made to do one thing in our life," Clark says. "We have the ability to learn a new thing. Even if you don't know how to do it today, you can learn it."

"At a baseline, most of us can agree if you're going to be spending 40 or more hours per week doing something, it would be much nicer if you enjoyed it. It is a worthwhile goal to strive to make the changes necessary, whether that involves changing jobs or changing careers or reskilling in some way so that you are able to do things more easily or shift the focus of your job so that you are actually more likely to be in a position where you're taking pleasure in the things that you are spending your time doing."

The lesson: It's normal to be scared, but everyone deals with these dilemmas at a certain juncture. In the end, is it worth choosing happiness over living in a job that doesn't present challenges or personal growth?

The easy out for Darius Rucker would have been to stay in his lane. That lane would be the path he carved in the world of rock and roll. As the leading singer of the group Hootie and the Blowfish, Rucker took the music world by storm in the early 90s as the frontman, and the group won two Grammy Awards. The first of six studio albums, "Cracked Rear View" in 1994, remains the 19th best-selling album of all time in the United States.

Rucker could have played it safe, but he followed his original passion instead. Growing up, one of six children in Charleston, South Carolina, Darius fell in love with music after hearing his Mom, Carolyn, sing in the kitchen. "All I wanted to do since I was four was play music," Rucker told NBC's Willie Geist in a 2023 "Today" show interview.

Rucker's love of music was fostered as a show choir member at Middleton High School. Being a part of the "Middleton Singers" fueled his passion. "It was why I got up in the morning," Rucker told Dan Rather in 2024. "It was why I went to school; it was to be a part of that group that I thought was so great."

Darius would graduate from Middleton High School and attend the University of South Carolina. Still, after forming Hootie and the Blowfish and finding early success around campus, a turning point in his professional life came when he confided in his Mom while contemplating leaving school to blaze his trail in the music world.

Rucker told Geist when he nervously told his Mom he wanted to drop out, his mother Carolyn gave him the backing he needed, telling him, "If that's what you want to do, do it."

While Rucker's mom passed before all of his musical fame and fortune, her son succeeded in the rock and roll world but then pivoted to an unfamiliar path for black artists: the world of country music.

Was he scared? Geist asked Rucker on his pivot from rock to country.

"An understatement," Rucker replied, noting he immediately felt pushback from music executives. "Three radio station executives said to my face, 'I don't think your audience will ever accept a black country singer.'"

Instead of being scared to pivot, Rucker was inspired to prove them wrong and forge his path, telling Geist, "That was more motivating for me. How hard do I have to work? Tell me what I have to do to make this work."

Darius Rucker grew up a country music fan. His musical idols were Kenny Rogers and Charley Pride, the first black member of the Grand Ole Opry and the first black artist to have a number-one country record.

Rucker's first country music record was number one on the charts, and he would go on to produce eight number-one hits and win four Grammy awards.

He still gets nervous when he begins every performance, but Darius Rucker fought the fear to make a defining pivot in his musical career.

"Once I made it, I wanted to see other people make it," Rucker told Geist.

PIVOTING TO SUCCESS (MAKING THE "BRAVE" JUMP)

Pat Clarke knows the feeling. You could make a case Clarke is the most popular sportscaster in the history of the Orlando media market. He spent 34 years as the lead sports anchor at Orlando's ABC & NBC affiliates. Still, in the underbelly of his broadcasting talents, Clarke always had a passion for cooking that he hoped to capitalize on.

Clarke may have been the top dog in Orlando for years, but growing up in tiny Colfax, Iowa, a city populated by just over two thousand people, he was always outnumbered. It was Clarke, his parents, and five sisters. "I still have physical and mental scars from my childhood," Clarke says with the dry humor that made him a successful sportscaster.

After realizing he wasn't going to make the big leagues while playing baseball at St. Ambrose University of Iowa, Clarke pivoted early on to his passion for talking and cooking. He took on play-by-play assignments while also hosting "Pat's Recipe Roundup" for a radio station 10 miles from his hometown.

"I had a Better Homes and Garden cookbook where I was just reading recipes, telling people we had tried these out at the KCOB test kitchen," Clarke said. "But it was all a ruse. We didn't even have a hot plate."

It was a rough broadcasting debut for Pat. During his first three weeks on the air, "no one called in with a recipe," Clarke remembered. Not even Clarke's mom and sister, who lived just down the road. But Clarke's broadcasting skills matured. He eventually transitioned to TV, getting on-air work and moving up the ladder in his home state with stops in Des Moines and Cedar Rapids before landing his big break as the main sports anchor in Orlando. From 1986 to 2019, he soaked in his passion for covering sports, but he never let go of his love for those culinary pursuits. He would carry it in the back of his mind for years.

The Goop Dog.

Clarke's mom, Betty, was a terrific cook who loved spicy food, but she was careful to relegate the amount of heat because she was sensitive to how it would affect her kids. Betty's answer to a chili dog back then was a beef-based sauce with brown sugar and baked beans served over a hot dog. Because the sauce was an on-the-fly concoction made with available ingredients, Betty appropriately dubbed it a Goop Dog.

By the time Clarke was in high school, he had seen it had become a household favorite. "Goodness knows how many Goop Dogs my sisters and I—and our friends—enjoyed," he said. Clarke and his mom had cooking and their love of Goop Dogs in common. "She taught me the rudimentary parts of cooking, and it became a passion," he said.

Clarke eventually saw this passion as a career opportunity. Yet he needed to add his personal touch to this family delicacy. The son would add some spice to Mom's original recipe to give it more flavor.

"I had an itch to give the pups a little more punch," he said, "so I toyed with different spices to add to Mom's creation. In full mad scientist mode, I ultimately found what those who love the Goop Dog today would say is a perfect combination of sweet and light heat."

Goop Dogs became so tasty to those who ate them that many implored Clarke to remove the hot dog so they could enjoy more Goop with each bite.

Betty's unique creation, perfected by her only son, became Clarke's growing passion. During his sportscasting career, a local Orlando pizza chain sold Pat's Goop Dogs with great success and rave reviews. Even before arriving in Orlando, Clarke remembers thinking of how he could bring the Goop Dogs to life.

"I knew at a point when I was in Cedar Rapids that this was something I wanted to do someday," he said. "I didn't know what the venue would be. I toyed with, 'Do I open up a bar and call it Pat Clarke's Press Box?' That idea always went through my mind."

Eventually, he went for it and took the scary plunge from the bright lights of sports media to selling Goop Dogs, but Clarke knew the timing was right when his contract wasn't renewed in 2019.

"That's when I said maybe things do happen for a reason," Pat said. "I believe in fate, so I started putting plans together to start selling at low-risk venues such as Farmer's Markets, just to see how it goes."

The pandemic put his plans on hold, but Pat saw it as a positive because it gave him more time to work on how to set them in motion. When he was finally able to launch the sale of Goop Dogs, they became an instant hit.

"Universally, people liked them if not loved them," he said.

Clarke enjoyed the initial exposure but then built on it by using the experience he gained as a sportscaster for years to launch his new venture into gooptastic frenzy, where the marketing aspect felt natural, as this former broadcast journalist had enjoyed being a storyteller for decades.

"Using the skills I have as an editor and to tell stories allows me to (control) my marketing," he said. "I know exactly what I want in my head."

The former sportscaster turned entrepreneur launched a website (goopdog.com) that featured clever themes for Valentine's Day, Mother's Day, Halloween, Thanksgiving, and Christmas. The career communicator effectively spread the word to the masses.

"You're letting people know what it is," he said. "You're letting them see other people try them too."

The guru of Goop hosted "Goop Gab" sessions with select Orlando VIPs from his home. Those sessions soon became a hit online and on social media. Clarke also created "Goop Gear," including hats and t-shirts, adding complimentary culinary delights such as his patented fried egg sandwiches and Betty's legendary caramel corn.

Clarke's marketing abilities transferred from TV to Goop Dogs, as did another commonality: his love for people. The transitions were applicable when establishing relationships with sports personalities in his prior career to now Goop fans at various events, from markets to weddings or charity events.

"You can engage yourself and endear yourself to them to the extent they may have not otherwise tried your product," he said. "Being able to talk to people, I enjoy people. I think that has helped as well."

Clarke transformed himself from a household name in Orlando as a sportscaster to a successful entrepreneur in a short amount of time. Having dreamed of a new career for years, seeing it come to life was liberating.

"The passion has been there for a long, long time," he said. "I always wanted to do this. I thought, 'Now is the time to do this, and you don't want to be old and decrepit and unable to move with a good mind and think, Gosh, I never did that one thing that I wanted to do.'

"At least now, I'm taking this thing out for a spin, and it's been so much fun. I have not had a bad weekend."

Doing something you're scared of isn't easy, but Clarke was passionate about his Goop Dreams. While he will forever appreciate everything his first career gave him, his second career has been equally, if not more fulfilling.

"It's very different because I've always worked for the man," he said. "I always worked for someone. Now I'm my own boss."

Overcoming the scary transition from years of success at one job to the unknowns of another gave Clarke a liberating feeling he appreciated.

"You really are kind of out there on an island, so you have to extend your tentacles, and I have no problem doing it using contacts that I made through my sportscasting," he said. "I find that to be very helpful."

Using the tools and contacts from his first passion to pivot to a newfound success was worth everything for this Founder of Goop.

"It's long hours on weekends, but it's so rewarding when you see people eat that sandwich and enjoy it, then come back and get more and leave a nice comment," he said. "Not all of them remember me from when I was on TV, but some do, and it's nice to hear what they have to say. So, this is a nice combo platter right now."

What does Clarke say to those reading this book and wondering why they should pursue a newfound career built on their passion?

"You have to do it because you don't want to grow old and be sitting around saying, 'Geez, I really wish I would have tried that,' because I can't imagine what that feeling would be like," he said.

Clarke has successfully pivoted his passion where big plans are ahead, and a possible slogan is in place: "You may not eat Goop Dogs every day, but you will want to."

CHAPTER TWO

MAXIMIZE RELATIONSHIPS

"Personal relationships are the fertile soil from which all advancement, all success, all achievement in real life grows."
Ben Stein

Once upon a time, teenager Lisa Kudrow was a biology major at Vassar College, a private liberal arts school in Poughkeepsie, New York.

At that point in her life, Kudrow had a game plan. The goal was to follow the career path of her dad and brother, who had gone to medical school. Her early love of medicine and science took hold in high school when she fell in love with her biology course.

Early on, the future actor and star of the iconic "Friends" show never acted in high school or college but leaned on her passion for biological theories.

Kudrow's pivot from biology to the big stage happened the summer before her senior year at Vassar when she noticed little things from the entertainment world that bothered her and made her think she could do better.

It irritated her to the point that she wanted to replace those doing the acting.

Years later, Kudrow delivered the commencement speech at her alma mater, and touched on that pivotal moment in her life.

The turning point in her potential pivot happened when she drove around LA the summer before her final year in college. She heard a promo for a sitcom on the radio. "I would remember hearing in my head, 'Oh God, that's not funny. They punched that joke too hard. Remember to throw it away when you do it,'" Kudrow told herself.

The attraction to performing wasn't an isolated incident. Kudrow started noticing aspects of performers everywhere, including late-night talk shows. "Those kinds of things kept coming up and happening like David Letterman. I would see someone on (and think), 'She seems too phony,'" Kudrow said on the Kelly Clarkson Show.

Kudrow couldn't deny her fascination with how performers perform and what she would do were she in those same situations. She would tell herself, "Lisa, when you are on Letterman, don't be phony." And then she would think to herself, "Why would I ever be on David Letterman?"

Little would she know what the future would hold.

Kudrow imagined herself as a performer, yet couldn't decide on a career path outside of the medical world.

Even though she couldn't shake the itch to perform, she started working with her Dad at a headache clinic. It is ironic because Kudrow's head was consumed with all the possibilities of what her life may be like in a different field – acting. It was a notion that wouldn't go away.

"I really got relentless," Kudrow told the Vassar graduates in her commencement speech. "So, I entertained the idea of being an actress."

Internally, she wanted to make a move, and she justified it, as crazy as the notion was. Unmarried and with no kids, now was the time, she thought. Despite just completing her biology degree, Kudrow got her family's support to go for it.

As discussed in Chapter One, being scared is normal for most pivoters. The fear factor consumed Kudrow initially, but there was a caveat. "I was a little terrified, but this didn't exactly feel like it was a choice as much as succumbing to a compulsion. I just listened to that inner voice," she said in her Vassar speech.

At that point, maximizing relationships became crucial to her success. After taking acting classes and getting a role in a local theater production, Kudrow started getting close to big breaks, but the consolation prize was building a solid network of friends.

While Kudrow was performing for the prestigious Groundlings Theatre and School in Los Angeles, "Saturday Night Live" creator and producer Lorne Michaels came to town to cast a female for SNL. The competition was future comedic stars Kathy Griffin and Julia Sweeney. Michaels picked Sweeney.

While rejection was tough and made Kudrow doubt her career pivot, building relationships with Griffin and Sweeney and her early mentor, future late-night host Conan O'Brien, kept her spirits up during these tough times.

Those early relationships' good thoughts and vibes kept Kudrow going through many rejections, close calls, and firings. Kudrow was fired from the show "Frasier" after only two days on set. At that point, she felt like giving up what seemed like a pointless pivot. "It was really hard to think that it wasn't meant to be. It was so embarrassing."

However, the close relationships with her peers helped keep the dream alive.

The lesson: Surround yourself with a supportive inner circle. Lean on those who, at the core, believe in your talents but will be honest with you about your next moves.

The support system eventually got Kudrow on the superstar trek to "Friends" fame. After getting fired from Frasier, she was nearly broke, and the only offer on the table was a small role as a waitress on the show, "Mad About You."

Kudrow's agent advised her not to take it as the producers demanded she audition in an hour to claim her role. Her agent thought it was a bad move, and she was above this treatment.

Her instincts told Kudrow that this was an opportunity she couldn't pass up. "I didn't think twice; of course, I took it," she said. "Whatever it is, I'll make it funny. I'll listen and respond."

Trusting her instincts and leaning on relationships gave Kudrow the green light to move forward at the turning point of her pivot. By taking the small waitress role on "Mad About You," the dominoes started to fall in her favor.

She made an impression as the waitress and was hired for five more episodes. The extended look would eventually give Kudrow the break of her career as one of the lead writers referred Lisa to his boyfriend, who recommended Kudrow try out for a new show called "Friends."

Relationships carried this young actor through tough times, and once Kudrow could showcase her talent, her growing network propelled her to the big time.

According to Kudrow, years later, one of the early producers of "Friends," Jim Burroughs, provided needed perspective. One day, Burroughs, Kudrow and the cast of "Friends" were exchanging collective war stories of what they went through to get to the show, when Burroughs intervened and told Kudrow, "Well, she's got the worst one of them all; she got fired from 'Frasier.'"

The ultimate pivot from Biology major to acting critic to actor wasn't easy, but the journey for Lisa Kudrow proved rewarding. Getting fired from "Frasier," being passed over for "Saturday Night Live" and countless other misses were all part of the journey that took her from the medical world to one of the most-watched TV shows ever. "They were actually all like guideposts that kept me on my path."

Believing in yourself matters, but maximizing the relationships in your life can help you embrace your passion and pivot to opportunities you could only dream of.

Meeting new people is something I've always enjoyed. Much to my daughter's chagrin, I tend to talk to everyone and sincerely appreciate idle conversation. (I'm kidding, girls!)

The world of sports television can be superficial, but the allure for me was never TV; it was my love of sports. After getting into the business, however, I quickly found that the main attraction was developing relationships with a variety of personalities—interesting, quirky, guarded, yet genuine people. I enjoyed the complete smorgasbord.

Many of these relationships were built with those going through the same experiences I had endured. Working in local news early on, we weren't paid much, had stressful jobs, and wondered if this career would be sustainable. In those days, having peers within your inner circle was invaluable and often therapeutic. Many of those relationships got me through those days and have stood the test of time.

Even though you are doing something you love, forming that inner circle is vital to your success.

Those personal relationships were important, but I immediately saw the value of growing my professional network. The development originated with the melting pot of high school coaches I covered during my first job in Tuscaloosa. To this day, I sometimes forget my address, yet remarkably, I still remember all those coaches' names. It's been decades since our paths crossed, yet those relationships meant so much to me. I enjoyed talking to them before practices and learning more about their players and who they were, their jobs, where they had been, and where they wanted to go with their careers. It was all fascinating to me. This collection of coaches was all so different, and it made it fun to cover their teams every week. I miss the simplicity of those days a great deal.

As my career progressed, I started identifying more with players, many of whom, at least early on in my career, were of a similar age. One player who taught me a lot about the importance of making quality relationships was a linebacker from Florida A&M University named Earl Holmes. He was the best player on the Rattlers and one of the best nationally. When I arrived in Tallahassee, Earl was poised for a breakout season, but there was one obstacle: he didn't trust the media. I immediately welcomed the challenge to gain his trust. When I first approached Earl, I told him, "Just give me one chance, and if I ever burn you, you'll never have to talk with me again." Holmes slowly let me in, and we developed a great relationship that extended to his family. I was the only reporter who sat with him on Draft Day, and I'll never forget hearing someone yell my name at a gas station years later. It was Earl's Mom who was driving a brand-new Mercedes, one of many great moments with the Holmes Family.

Getting to know Earl Holmes provided valuable lessons on how to be a better reporter. You remain objective but must be fair when earning the trust of those you cover regularly. This doesn't mean you tolerate rude behavior or pander to them, but in building great relationships, it's essential to listen and learn everything you can about someone. It allows them to understand you and know your true intentions. There is no timetable for this, but being sincere and showing others you have no agenda is vital. In subsequent years, I valued the trust I earned with various players and coaches, which made my stories better and subsequently made their stories better. Because of the trust we developed, the players and coaches opened up more and provided information they would not have shared with others. Earning their trust and developing relationships was the part of the job I enjoyed the most. I liked the challenge and was fascinated to learn all the different facets about them that made them unique.

As a young sports anchor in my second TV stop in Tallahassee, Florida, I started my "Naborhood" show to get to know sports personalities away from conventional and often stifling media atmospheres such as press conferences and locker rooms. The format I created would have me invite a player or coach to co-host the sportscast with me. They would read off the teleprompter, do highlights, and we would always produce a funny skit each week. Along the way, I learned much about how to foster relationships better. One example taught me how you sometimes need hustle and luck to succeed.

It was 1998, and Florida State University was bringing an old man— 25-year-old freshman quarterback Chris Weinke—onto its football team. Weinke had accepted a scholarship from FSU back in 1990 but chose instead to pursue a baseball career after being drafted in the second-round of the Major League Baseball draft by the Toronto Blue Jays. Seven years later, while standing at the doorstep of the major leagues as Triple-A infielder/outfielder, Weinke decided to return to play football in Tallahassee.

In those days, Florida State was one of the best programs in the country. The competition was everywhere, even for Weinke, who was battling Dan Kendra for the starting quarterback job. Kendra had been the number one recruit in the country, could throw the ball a mile, and lifted more weight than most linebackers. He had it all, and I wanted him to be my guest in the "Naborhood." But FSU's sports information office said I couldn't get Kendra and would have to settle for Weinke. I didn't want it, but I figured we would make it work anyway.

What happened over the next few days was an incredible twist of fate.

Our show was on Sunday, but in the days before that, Kendra injured his knee during FSU's spring football game, and Weinke was thrust into the starter's role. Suddenly, the oldest quarterback in college football was the oldest "starting" quarterback, and I would get my first extensive interview with him. Weinke's appearance in the "Naborhood" went great. He was funny and mature enough to handle everything we threw at him. Even better, his appearance gave the show credibility with his FSU teammates, who took notice and became eager to come to the show themselves.

That appearance is where Weinke and I laid the foundation for a great relationship built on trust. The relationship allowed me to get several exclusive interviews after leaving Tallahassee and moving on to my next job in Jacksonville. Weinke and I did many stories that other reporters couldn't have done. As for Weinke, he became the oldest college football player to win the Heisman Trophy and later became an NFL and college coach. We remain friends even today, and it all started on that fateful Sunday in Tallahassee in the "Naborhood."

Life is funny. While Weinke won almost every award a college football quarterback could win that season, Purdue's Drew Brees often finished runner-up. Ironically many years later an encounter with Brees would change my career.

That relationship developed much like my relationship with Weinke, through hustle sprinkled with a little luck.

I started covering the New Orleans Saints in 2006, a year after Hurricane Katrina had ravaged the Big Easy. While the city was undergoing a massive rebuild, so was its football team. The reset included a new head coach, Sean Payton, and a new quarterback, Brees. During their first year together, with a rebuilt roster, Payton, Brees, and the Saints impressively made the NFC Championship game for the first time in team history. That season, I interviewed Brees a lot, but never one-on-one.

That soon changed.

After the season, I went to Walt Disney World to interview Drew for a promotional shoot following the Pro Bowl. The only two outlets were Cox Sports Television (CST), a cable network in New Orleans that I represented, and ESPN. We went first, but once Drew wrapped up his session with ESPN, I heard him tell one of the producers, "If you ever need to contact me, call my marketing agent, Chris Stuart." I didn't have a notepad, but my videographer had a Sharpie. I quickly eavesdropped, wrote Stuart's number on my hand, and later put it on paper.

It was one of the best moves of my career.

What followed was an incredible series of events. First, I was in San Diego the following weekend, working on a documentary of Saints then-rookie running back, Reggie Bush. Brees' marketing agent, Chris Stuart, whom I had called that week, was ironically based in San Diego. After wrapping up the Bush shoot, I was in my hotel when Stuart randomly called me. I was hoping he would sign off on a Brees documentary, but as it turned out, he wanted much more.

Stuart told me he had brokered deals with several other clients who were major league baseball players and partnered them with cable companies like the one I was working for. They had put together several creative deals where the networks would have the players and their wives review movies and have the players do various segments for the sports networks. Stuart wondered, "Is that something I would be interested in?"

I almost dropped my cell phone.

After connecting Stuart with my bosses at Cox Sports Television, a deal was agreed upon to have Brees do a show with me after every game—preseason, regular season, and playoffs. At the time, I thought this would be great for a few years, but Drew and I did those segments for 14 seasons, racking up nearly 300 one-on-one interviews together. Then, after Brees retired, he signed off on a deal where I could use all of our interviews for my first book, "The Brees Way," which outlined our best conversations.

This was all a result of me grabbing a Sharpie and writing a phone number on my hand!

Maximizing relationships doesn't mean taking advantage of anybody. It means discovering the best route to get the most out of someone in a way that benefits you both. Whether it was the high school coaches I covered early in my career, understanding why Earl Holmes didn't trust the media, or working hard to build trust with Weinke and Brees, maximizing relationships made me a better reporter and enabled those I worked with to feel more comfortable.

Getting the most out of your relationships shouldn't just be a goal in your personal life. To succeed at anything you do, maximizing your relationships with those you interact with is imperative. My reporting examples can serve as a template for your vocation. If you sell real estate, go the extra mile and get creative to make your clients comfortable. If you're an attorney, be sure that those you represent or future clients know you're not a phony and have their best interests in mind. We have all dealt with doctors who could possess better people skills to cultivate better relationships. When you maximize your relationships, you maximize your ability to succeed in life at whatever you may pursue. Building relationships makes you more effective and adds more passion to your purpose.

PIVOTING TO SUCCESS (VIA BUILDING RELATIONSHIPS)

Jason Alpert always had a knack for adlibbing. As a young sportscaster in his first job out of college, he anchored a local sportscast when a videographer accidentally walked by and kicked a studio camera during his live local show. The camera started shaking, but as he read his sportscast, Alpert rolled with it, never flinching. Then, when the cameras stopped shaking, Alpert quickly mimicked the camera and shook a little bit on-air himself to make fun of the moment.

The gesture received rave reviews from friends watching from home and several colleagues in the newsroom, but his boss wasn't amused. "Afterward, the general manager came into the sports office and said, 'Don't ever call attention to your mistakes like that. Just go on and keep doing it.'"

The moment stuck with Alpert for years and carried over to what would turn out to be his true calling and defining pivot, a benefit auctioneer. His former boss may not have deemed his on-air reaction appropriate. Still, Alpert's ability to maneuver around obstacles was the perfect skill set for his second career, where being ready for anything is a prime prerequisite.

"That's one thing that stuck in my head because now we lean into everything that happens," Alpert said. "It is live on stage, and we will work with whatever is thrown our way. I felt like you're performing a little bit when you're on TV, but in a box. You have the script. You have your rundown, and you do what you have to do. What we do now, it's much more live theatre, improv theatre."

Alpert's successful pivot from sportscaster to one of the most successful benefit auctioneers has him looking back at that early moment in his TV career with a fresh and liberating perspective.

"I think about that moment a lot," he said. "Now, I get to do whatever I want."

Pivoting towards your second passion can be liberating, but the road to the promised land wasn't easy for Jason. After rising up the ranks of local television markets, he hit a few bumps. Across ten years, he averaged a new job every year, and his life as a sportscaster was taking its toll. Though he loved what he did, Jason had a decision to make when his regional network folded while living in South Florida.

"I had a choice at that point," he said. "I could have stayed in sportscasting and continued my career in another city, but I said, 'You know what, I want to find something else to do.' It was kind of the jumping-off point."

So how did Alpert transform his career from sportscaster to auctioneer? Let's say the new career found him instead of him finding it. The first step was accepting a job as Marketing Manager for Homestead-Miami Speedway, home of NASCAR, Indy Car, and the Rolex Grand-Am Series. Quickly, Jason applied all the skills that made him a successful sportscaster for his next career, a lesson for anyone pivoting from one passion to the next.

First and foremost, Jason was comfortable with a microphone in his hand. He had proven that on the air in sports. After initially being asked to hire the PA announcers, Alpert would eventually emcee the pre- and post-race shows at Homestead. His duties included introducing the National Anthem, the flyover, trophy presentations, and everything but the actual racing. In addition, the track had Alpert hosting all of its mobile marketing efforts, further showcasing his talents.

"They knew I was comfortable with a crowd, comfortable with a microphone, which certainly comes from my TV career," he said.

After working at Homestead for three years, Alpert faced a big obstacle. His scope had seemingly expanded to a new opportunity where he could use his skills to promote athlete's charity events. Still, when he reported for his first day of work, he found the connection who had hired him had been fired, and his new job was no longer available. Jason subsequently asked for his job back, but their policy was not to rehire anyone who had quit. Homestead Speedway appreciated Alpert's versatility, though, and valued his ability to roll with any punch thrown his way. So, when an opening for a public address announcer for the track came, he was seen as the perfect candidate. Alpert's hustle paid off as he became the voice of the races, calling all the action for those in attendance, and he was poised for the challenge. Within a year, he had worked his way up the ladder from doing only small races to doing PA for all the Homestead races, eventually acquiring the name "Voice of NASCAR."

It was a position he held for the next eight years, but the funny thing is that Alpert continued searching for his true calling. While handling PA duties at the track, Alpert dabbled in sportscasting on the side. Then a turning point came for Jason when after seeing his work on a consistent basis, Homestead began referring him to host several events in the area. After proving himself, he was offered similar jobs outside of South Florida. That side business grew to a point where he worked for the Indy Car Series, building content and hosting live events on their respective Jumbotron screens. It went so well that Alpert went on the road with the Indy Car Series for 17 weeks.

The tipping point in his pivot came at a much smaller venue. A few years later, Alpert was hired to emcee a charity event for Summit Christian School in West Palm Beach, Florida. He had planned on being the emcee, but those plans changed when the auctioneer failed to show.

When asked by the event organizers if he did auctions, Alpert said, "Of course, I do auctions," even though he had never done an auction in his life.

"But it went pretty well, and afterward, they asked me to do their events as an auctioneer," Alpert said. "From there, it just kind of grew."

Before we get to how much it grew, there are many valuable takeaways from Alpert's pivotal journey:

- **Have confidence in your abilities:** Alpert had no auctioneer experience, but his background gave him the confidence to do the job, leading to his success. Know your strengths and know when to use them to create new options.
- **Seize your moment:** Alpert could have been happy with a good night at the office, but he saw the big picture. He was a successful emcee, but opening the door to being an auctioneer promised more work and the potential for a new career.
- **Do something you're scared of:** Alpert was confident enough to accept the challenge and overcame the fear that he could fail miserably. Not only did he not fail, but his success led to opportunities beyond his wildest imagination.

Today, Jason runs Alpert Enterprises, which provides benefit auctioneers for charity fundraisers. In addition, "We are fundraising consultants," he said. "Actually, we are first and foremost fundraising consultants/ benefit auctioneers."

That tiny event at Summit Christian School opened up a new world for Alpert, and to his credit, he pivoted and took full advantage of it. He started his company in 2007 as more of a side hustle, but "Alpert Enterprises" boasts a full-time staff of auctioneers who work more than 200 events a year. And that company is growing by leaps and bounds each year.

Alpert made the leap in making his auctioneer side hustle his full-time job at a vulnerable time in his life. He had recently married, and his wife was six months pregnant with their first child. At the time, they only had seven charity events on the docket. But…

Failing wasn't an option. Creating options changed Alpert's career and his life. He bet on himself because he believed in himself!

"Ultimately, to be forced to be successful, whatever that was going to look like, was imperative," he said. "I knew I was never going to live in a van down by the river. I was going to make it work one way or another. Whether it was doing this charity thing, whether it was emceeing, whether it was videography, or public address announcing, I was going to form that into something."

Alpert has built his company into a nationwide success that proved durable even during the Coronavirus pandemic when he switched from live to virtual auctions online.

"I hate to say this, but it was a relatively seamless transition from doing our in-person events to doing these virtual events because of our TV background," he said. "All we were doing was putting on virtual fundraising TV shows. The model that Jerry Lewis had for 50 years for the Muscular Dystrophy Association with their Labor Day telethon, that's all we were doing. We were just doing it online."

Alpert's continued success through the pandemic is proof that we can all pivot to new successes and happiness by using the skills we've acquired over time.

Jason and his team of auctioneers, many of whom had similar television backgrounds, adapted. They followed their old television foundation of creating rundowns and producing shows with dressed-up opens, transitions, and an occasional produced commercial to garner great results.

"As a company, we did 110 virtual fundraisers," Alpert said.

The bottom line was good for both parties, as his company was still collecting its normal rate. Meanwhile, the virtual experience was far less expensive for the organizations, as they didn't need to pay for a venue, band, or catering. It was a pandemic win-win.

It is a profitable win-win, but Alpert still prefers his standard business model, which leans on his passion.

"I would tell you that I would never choose to go back to that," he said of the virtual auctions. "We did it because we had to, but what I crave, what I love, is the energy from the crowd. Having 500 people in front of you, hanging on every word you say, and applauding when you are successful in doing what you are trying to do is what I love, and that's what I missed. You don't get that on local TV. You don't get that in virtual fundraising. You get that being on stage at an in-person charity event."

Alpert found his new voice and pivoted towards a passion that proved there was life after television. His new love has him in arenas he never could have imagined, performing all over the country, in front of thousands of people and alongside big names such as country singer Carrie Underwood, Jay Leno and John Legend. He has become a success because he loves his work and has found a new outlet.

"That's a huge part of it," he said. "You can look at it both ways. I like it because I'm good at it, but I'm also good at it because I like it."

That's the essential message of this book: Do what you like, and you will reap the rewards. Alpert followed his passion and then pivoted to something he grew to love even more because he used all of his resources.

"I'm a performer, an entertainer first and foremost," said Alpert, who has helped hundreds of charities raise millions of dollars, all while having fun doing it.

"We're going to come in and raise you a ton of money, but we're also going to put on a great show," he said. "I think I'm good at it because I can control the crowd. I know how to ask and not beg."

Alpert's acquired skill set is displayed because he built on his passion.

"Some of that comes from my career in TV, where you had to be compelling with a microphone in your hand and explain why people should care, and that's what I do every night now," he said.

Many of you reading this book may think, "But I'm not a performer. I'm not comfortable speaking in front of a crowd. But I do have a passion. How do I make the pivot to change my life?"

Alpert gives this advice: "You gotta take that first step. You gotta crawl before you walk and walk before you run. I was so scared for so long to do those things."

Overcoming something you're scared of is a common refrain in this book and an emotion we all share, but many of us don't act on it. Alpert did and discovered the rewards, but that doesn't mean the decisions we make in pivoting aren't reversible.

"This is something that comes from my Dad that he shared with me when I was a teenager and still holds with me today," Alpert said in passing on his last piece of advice. "There is no decision you make in life besides birth and death that you can't change. If you leave sportscasting, if you leave the TV business and fail at what you're trying to do, go back."

You can always go back.

Alpert may never return to television as his business is thriving, but his message is important. Pivoting to your passion doesn't mean you can't return to your original vocation. Your pivot can create either temporary or long-lasting freedom. Either way, it's a viable option to do whatever you are passionate about. The bottom line is that finding something that fulfills you enables you to handle the ups and downs while building on your success. Alpert walked away from his dream and created a new one, a leap of faith that paid off financially and emotionally. The change has been liberating.

"The fact that I am successful at it, we get off the stage, and we know that we just raised a tremendous amount of money and put on a great show makes it so much easier to put up with the hard work that goes into it," he said. "In our first ten years, we've raised a quarter of a billion dollars for charities, and by the end of 2024 will eclipse the 350 million raised threshold. The numbers get staggering when you start calculating them."

Alpert's creation has helped hundreds of charities financially, and he and his family have also reaped the benefits. This is a stark contrast to all of the jobs Jason endured before starting his company.

"Especially financially," Alpert said. "When you're in TV and making $20,000, $30,000, $40, 000 or maybe $50,000 per year, we're thrilled with it. Now I have found something that drives me, that I still love doing, and fuels me where I can set my family up for success in the future."

Raising the bar of his professional career was all Jason Alpert's doing. He overcame several difficult years in television and bet on himself and his skill set to create something his own. In the process, he created a better life for himself than he ever imagined he'd have.

"Twenty years ago, if you tried to map out where I was going to be and what I would do," he said, "this wasn't even on the radar."

CHAPTER THREE

MAKE YOUR TRIP!

"Travel isn't always pretty. It isn't always comfortable. Sometimes, it hurts; it even breaks your heart. But that's OK. The journey changes you; it should change you. It leaves marks on your memory, on your consciousness, on your heart, and your body. You take something with you. Hopefully, you leave something good behind."
Anthony Bourdain

PASSION CHASER

For renowned musician Dave Grohl it was a "pivotal" trip indeed.

A 700-mile, 11-hour trek from his childhood home of Springfield, Virginia, to Evanston, Illinois.

A summer trek that would change his life forever.

Young Dave Grohl had grown up loving music, but on this trip, that love would manifest into a passion that would fuel one of the most iconic careers in the music world's history.

That event unfolded one evening while Grohl was out with friends at a bar across the street from Wrigley Field called the Cubby Bear Lounge.

What Grohl saw that night was something he had never experienced: a punk rock music frenzy where the crowd was so in tune with the band Naked Raygun, that it was transformed into a sea of slam dancing. Grohl was also shoved, but it didn't bother him a bit. It was a game-changer, as he described in his biography, "Dave Grohl, The Storyteller."

"This was a feeling of freedom that I had waited for my entire life, and now that I'd been baptized by spit and sweat and broken glass, there was no turning back," Grohl said.

Finding your passion is powerful, and Grohl found his at an early age when that moment altered his life. "In one summer day," he said, "I was forever changed."

Grohl's career would eventually see him take numerous trips around the country, searching for success in the music world. His revealing biography chronicles his journey after dropping out of high school. He traveled around the country, spending a lot of time in the back of vans, on floors of houses and hotels, and in sleeping bags until he made it.

Reading "The Storyteller" reminded me that Grohl, who eventually became one of the best performers in the world, made it because he loved the craft—everything about it. His love for music got him through the tough times and enabled him to endure the seemingly endless road trips on his journey to the top.

Sure, Grohl has gifts many of us don't have. The difference is he acted on them. He wasn't a trained musician then, but he worked through many obstacles to become successful simply because of his love for music. It wasn't about the money, though that would eventually come. But the money came because he was doing what he loved, and it showed.

As he writes in "The Storyteller," "By the time music got its hooks in me, I became hopelessly preoccupied with every aspect of its construction, throwing all other childhood interests out the window."

One of the stories in Grohl's book, which many can relate to, dates back to when he was in high school. Grohl was not a good student, so his prospects outside of music were slim. He was fortunate then to have been offered a break with the band "Scream." Accepting the opportunity meant dropping out of school, which his father strongly advised against. Grohl's mother saw things differently. She was more supportive of Dave's dream, so when this son of divorced parents asked his mother if he could drop out of school and tour the world, she responded more favorably, yet bluntly.

"You better be good," she said. (It was an exchange reminiscent of the one Darius Rucker had with his Mom, which propelled his career.)

A supportive push from his inner circle was all Grohl needed. His Mom's warning amounted to a yes for the young musician. Soon thereafter, Grohl dropped out of school and became a success beyond his and her wildest dreams, eventually evolving into a transformative musical talent as the drummer for the legendary rock band Nirvana. Later, after the death of Nirvana lead singer Kurt Cobain, Grohl continued to make his mark, making the rare pivot to become lead singer and songwriter for one of the most popular rock bands in the world, the Foo Fighters.

IT CAME DOWN TO THIS: I HAD TO MAKE THE TRIP.

After graduating from college, I thought finding a job in broadcasting would be easy. This mindset starkly contrasted the message most of my cynical professors (they would say realistic) had consistently relayed to me and my classmates. The job market varies for each graduating class, but for a budding sportscaster, the odds worsen yearly as hundreds, sometimes thousands, apply for almost every opening.

The funny part of this equation is this elusive opening didn't pay handsomely. It was all about the opportunity, the chance to break in.

The first resume tape I sent out elicited an immediate response, leading me to believe my first destination would be Nacogdoches, Texas. This city has a population of about 30,000 and is roughly the same size as my hometown of Titusville, Florida. Titusville is a few miles away from Kennedy Space Center on the eastern part of the state on Florida's Space Coast.

I'll never forget when the sports director of the brand-new Nacogdoches TV station called me and told me he wanted me to be the Weekend Sports Anchor and that they were offering to fly me out for an interview. I was ecstatic. Frankly, I didn't care where my first job was. I would have gone anywhere: Tacoma, Washington, Wheeling, West Virginia, or Nacogdoches, Texas!

Let's do this!

Then, a week later, I received a call that changed my life in the short term, yet helped me in the long run.

The Sports Director in Nacogdoches told me during that call that he wanted to hire me but that a media consultant hired by the station had concluded I looked too young. I was crushed. They voided my plane ticket, so the search for my first job was back on.

And on and on it went.

After that rejection, I looked and looked and looked for a job, but nothing materialized. I was a finalist for a few positions but couldn't land the big fish. In the interim, my parents were very supportive. After putting me through college, they seemed to believe in me more than ever. As the weeks and months went by, I contemplated grad school, law school, and giving up on the dream that had driven me since elementary school. I interned for the St Louis Cardinals in Spring Training, a job that didn't pay, but I finished second in the team's NCAA college basketball tournament pool, which paid $1,200. That helped make up for working every day for a month and a half for free!

At that point, my Dad gave me some of the best advice I'd ever received. He said, "Buddy, I think you should take a trip."

He wanted me to dub off a boatload of resume tapes, plot a trip around the country, and chase the elusive job. At first, I thought he was crazy, but the more I thought about it, the more excited I got about the prospects. I figured I would map out a large triangle in the middle of the United States chock full of several small and middle-size markets that would suit my skill set. I would compile a list of stations, phone numbers, and key contacts I could reach out to, call them a day or two before I was in town, and hope they would have a few minutes to meet with me, even though they didn't have an opening.

After dubbing off the tapes, my first stop from Tallahassee, Florida, was Anniston, Alabama. I remember waiting in the lobby to talk to the News Director. That same day, the news broke that basketball star Magic Johnson had been diagnosed as HIV-positive, and his press conference was being played live on a TV in the lobby. The news director was cordial; he met with me briefly but explained that he had no sports openings. I left thinking, 'You knew this wouldn't be easy.' It was time to grind.

I had designs on driving from Anniston to Minneapolis, Minnesota, then down to Lubbock, Texas, where a friend had just found work, before returning home. I made that trek, staying with friends or at a Red Roof Inn. Along the way, the Cardinals even put me up for a few days in St Louis, Chicago, and Houston, where I was hired for a few dollars to do stats.

I remember a News Director in Topeka, Kansas, telling me I had a speech impediment (I had never heard that before). I remember an encouraging word from the boss in Cedar Rapids, Iowa. I mainly remember many miles, a lot of self-doubt, and a sprinkle of hope that it would all be worth it.

Early on, that sprinkle was found in my second stop, Tuscaloosa, Alabama. It was the CBS station, the only station in town, with a market size of 180. The interview went great; the connection was sincere. I loved the city and felt it would be the right fit. They felt like they would have an opening but didn't know when it would become official.

After every interview, I drove and drove, thinking that while Tuscaloosa seemed like a perfect fit, I could not count on it as I continued my quest. I drove to Minneapolis and then down to Texas, returning home with many miles on my car and zero job prospects besides my lead in Alabama.

A few weeks later, I got the call from Tuscaloosa's sports director, telling me I was the choice and asking when I could start. I was ready to drive up there immediately! I started a few weeks later, right before football season, during which Alabama won its first national title in 13 years. I didn't cover a Crimson Tide loss for almost two years. It was the perfect place to start my career.

I always wonder how my life would have been different if I had gotten the Nacogdoches job. I think we all have a Nacogdoches scenario at some point. It could be a job, a relationship, or a pivotal moment we missed out on that changes everything and puts us on a different trajectory.

The lesson: When in doubt, when you think you're at a dead-end, or when you think you're perfect for a job, but there is a lot of competition, how do you separate yourself?

Make the trip!

You never know where life takes you. Sometimes, like Lisa Kudrow's acting journey or the heartbreak I felt not getting that initial job out of school, rejection can make you feel your big break will never happen.

That's why leaning on your relationships is vital, where "making the trip" is a metaphor for going the extra mile. My trip expanded my network and increased my odds of finding my dream career.

I wouldn't have gotten the Tuscaloosa job if I hadn't made the trip; I firmly believe that.

Six years later, I was a finalist for a job in Jacksonville, Florida, that I wanted badly. I knew what a big move it would be for my career. So, I returned to my roots and made another trip, albeit a much shorter one, as I was living just a few hours away in Tallahassee. I called the station to see if I could drop off another "updated" resume tape for the opening. They agreed and ultimately hired me.

For years afterward, the sports director in Jacksonville joked, "We hired Nabors because he made the trip." You know what they say. There's always a hint of truth in sarcasm.

Making the trip showed how badly I wanted the job and how hard I would work if I got it. It opened their eyes and showed how passionate I was about excelling. I've never lost that passion or my love for sportscasting, but I learned later that I would have to pivot to continue to enjoy my craft.

In my early years, I learned that you must find creative ways to get the desired job. For me, that meant making the trip.

MAKING THE TRIP IS PRICELESS FOR MANY

Grohl considered the many road trips and nights spent sleeping in sleeping bags worth it because he found his passion.

"There were certain things in my life that I relied on unconditionally. The unwavering love of my mother, my love for her, and the love that filled my heart when I played music," he later wrote in his book.

Do something you're scared of? Grohl is a shining example. He was still willing to take risks even after he'd made it. For example, before the 2016 Academy Awards, Grohl was asked to play the Beatles song "Blackbird" solo without the Foo Fighters. He admitted in his book that even after all the success he had achieved in his career, the thought of this challenge frightened him. At the same time, it strengthened his resolve as a musician.

"Courage is a defining factor in the life of any artist," Grohl writes in his autobiography. "The courage to bear your innermost feelings, to reveal your true voice, or to stand in front of an audience and lay it out there for the world to see.

"Will they like it? Am I good enough? It is the courage to be yourself that bridges those opposing emotions, and when it does, magic can happen."

The magic of finding what you want to do in this world is liberating. We should all strive for it. Some find it early, others later. The key is to know that it's never too late to begin the search.

For Dave Grohl, music took hold of him early, and the love of what he did for a living superseded any material gains. Because he loved his craft, his passion enabled his life to find success naturally.

"I decided to dive through it, leaving a life of stability and security behind," Grohl writes in "The Storyteller." "I was ready to be free. I was ready to bet everything on this burning passion that raged inside of me, and I committed to honor it."

Had he not followed his heart, Grohl could have lived an entirely different and possibly unfulfilling life. But he found something he loved, something he enjoyed working at. As his love continually fueled his passion, he got better and eventually became a great musician who has inspired thousands of others.

As he climbed toward the pinnacle of his profession, money and fame came, too, but Grohl achieved success, not for those goals. All those trips in the backs of buses and nights on the floor in sleeping bags were worth it because he followed his dreams, not dollar signs.

Years after making my trip, I enjoyed a reminder of how small this world is. At the time, I was working for Fox Sports Net Florida as one of their main reporters. It was the best job I ever had. One night, while covering an NBA playoff game in Milwaukee, I went out for a few drinks with some members of the Milwaukee media. One was a reporter who amazingly was the same one who got that Nacogdoches job that I so greatly coveted in college. We immediately became friends and still keep in touch. Each year on our birthdays, we wish each other "Happy Nacogdoches Day!"

I'll never know how my life would have been different if I would have gotten that job in Nacogdoches, but I do know how it turned out after taking a trip of a lifetime.

When in doubt, make the trip! It will be a life-changer; you never know where going the extra mile will lead you.

CHAPTER FOUR

IT'S OK TO QUIT, BUT YOU BETTER HAVE A PLAN!

"To improve is to change, so to be perfect is to have changed often."
Winston Churchill

Arnold Schwarzenegger's iconic line in his 1984 breakout movie, "The Terminator," was "I'll be back."

How ironic as his life was a series of, I'll be "backs."

In terms of pivoting, Schwarzenegger's life featured unprecedented zigzags, overcoming a myriad of obstacles to pivot from a former Mr. Universe in bodybuilding to a leading man on the big screen to ultimately governor of the state of California.

There has never been such a journey. Arnold's constant pivots personify the major tenets of this book.

Schwarzenegger's life passes on lessons in perseverance, hard work, and the ultimate pivot lesson: know no boundaries; use the skills you have acquired to move on to a passion that can bring you happiness you could have never imagined.

Who uses bodybuilding skills to move on to a career in acting? Who builds off being an action hero to find a career in politics?

The ultimate pivot success story is Arnold Schwarzenegger.

Born in Austria, Schwarzenegger soon developed an inner confidence that pushed him from an early age, as he outlined in his self-titled Netflix three-part series, "Arnold."

"My whole life I had this talent that I could see things very clearly in front of me. If I can see it, it must be achievable. Do things everyone calls impossible, and that gives you the will."

Schwarzenegger's innate drive provided a foundation for a "pivotal" career like we've never seen. "You can make your visions not only become a reality but go beyond your dreams. I had a fire in the belly for much more ... much ... much more," he outlined in his documentary.

Unlike Darius Rucker and Dave Grohl, Schwarzenegger didn't find support at home. His father didn't understand how anyone could make a living lifting weights and looking at themselves in the mirror. Arnold had to discover his inner circle beyond his home, where friends raised money for him to compete in bodybuilding contests, and many mentors took him under his wing to train with him, introduce him to the right people, and ultimately develop his skills.

Relationships are everything. Surround yourself with those who support your dreams and can build confidence, enabling you to move closer to your passion.

Once Schwarzenegger surrounded himself with the right people, his hard work was enhanced in many ways. At 20, he won Mr. Universe, the first of 13 world bodybuilding championships. This platform was rewarding but afforded him the chance for bigger things.

This budding star knew he had to "make the trip," realizing that moving to America would enhance his career and take him to places he couldn't have previously fathomed. Having the gumption to change and a supportive inner circle afforded Schwarzenegger better training techniques, a growing network of influence, and maybe most importantly, an atmosphere to improve his communication skills.

In his new homeland, Arnold took advantage of improving his speech through several English classes designed to position his bodybuilding platform as a conduit to his next pivot: acting.

Bodybuilding put Schwarzenegger on many people's radar, but this Mr. Universe wanted more, and he entered the entertainment waters unprepared.

In his first break, he changed his name to Arnold Strong for a role as Hercules, but he had never taken any acting classes, and it showed; the movie was a bomb and for a while, Schwarzenegger's movie career spiraled downward.

Five years came and went: no offers where the naysayers lined up against him. Agents, managers, and studio executives told Schwarzenegger he didn't fit the acting prototype. He was much too big and muscular and needed to work on his craft.

To get his feet wet, Arnold played roles he knew, he played a bodybuilder in "Stay Hungry," where he learned a lot from respected co-stars and veteran actors Sally Field and Jeff Bridges.

Schwarzenegger then starred in the popular documentary "Pumping Iron," which helped show Hollywood that he was gaining more of a comfort level when performing in front of the camera. The documentary was a hit at the prestigious Cannes Film Festival, which gave Arnold more notoriety.

Still, he couldn't find an agent to appreciate his rare talents.

The struggles continued, yet Schwarzenegger's confidence didn't wane. He didn't want to just play bodybuilding roles, in fact, he didn't want supporting roles; he was going for it all.

Director James Cameron said in the documentary "Arnold" that when he met Schwarzenegger and he auditioned for the role in his "Terminator" movie, he asked him to "tell me about your process as an actor." Arnold replied, "I don't want to be an actor, I want to be a star."

After sitting on the sidelines and starring in roles where he basically played himself, Schwarzenegger was better equipped for his second big break many years later as the lead in "Conan the Barbarian." This time, he prepared, doing all the stunts, which included hours of horseback riding. The movie was a huge box office hit and set the stage for his master pivot into Hollywood.

Schwarzenegger beat out O.J. Simpson for the lead role in "The Terminator," yet he still had his doubts. He didn't want to play a villain, and the part only had 26 lines. Cameron convinced him to take it, and the rest is history.

A pivot like we've never seen before.

Are you happy at work?

Are you passionate about what you do?

If you answered yes and yes, that's great, but you're in the minority. A Gallup poll in 2021 found that only 36% of U.S. employees are engaged in their work and workplace, which aligns with a composite poll by Gallup in 2020. Those results found that only 20% of global employees are engaged.

A revealing 2022 article in the Harvard Business Review by Marcus Buckingham, the head of people and performance research at the ADP Research Institute (ADPRI), titled "Designing Work That People Love," showcased this engagement problem in the workplace. Buckingham and his team's results further prove that most people aren't happy in their jobs. His findings concluded that most workers aren't passionate about their work.

Buckingham and his colleagues found through research at the ADPRI that people weren't happy with work, pandemic or no pandemic. Their studies concluded that before the pandemic, only 18% of respondents were fully engaged at work, 17% felt highly resilient, and 14% trusted their senior leaders and team leaders. Furthermore, this study highlighted that in 2021, a quarter of U.S. workers quit their jobs, the highest percentage in American history.

In addition, the Centers for Disease Control reported in 2018 that 71% of adults had at least one symptom of workplace stress, such as headaches or feeling overwhelmed or anxious.

This study by Buckingham and his colleagues concluded that "only when a company intelligently links what people love to their actual activities will it achieve higher performance, higher engagement, resilience, and lower turnover."

Any way you slice it, there is a lot of unhappiness at the workplace. There are many reasons for this, but I firmly believe your happiness is not predicated on your bosses' management style—it's something you can control. You control your happiness. You can stay or build a plan and either start something on your own or find a new employer who better appreciates your skill set.

This is on you—you have the power to pivot toward change!

Let's face it; we can't be happy all the time. We all get irritated sometimes, be it with our boss, co-workers, even our clients and customers. The book, "Why Do So Many Incompetent Men Become Leaders," by Tomas Chamorro-Premuzic, estimates the managerial incompetence scale is at least 50%. In this study, even the best of the best underperforms when they aren't managed by good leadership. This book postulates that this behavior won't change, so I agree with its contention that to fix your unhappiness, you need to form a plan to find happiness elsewhere. This book concludes, "Rather than continue waiting for your boss to get coached, or suddenly wake up with a personality transplant, consider looking for a better one."

To quit or not to quit?

How often do you encounter a co-worker's unhappiness at your job? We hear it all the time. Many feel compelled to stay, it's the safe move, yet the word "quit" often has negative connotations, and I get it. I don't want my children to quit unless they follow through with an activity, whether it's sports, a school play, or being a crossing guard. But when it comes to working, I think it's often healthy to quit—as long as you have a plan!

Merriam-Webster defines "quit" in several ways: "to give up employment (how appropriate) or to cease normal, expected, or necessary action, or to admit defeat."

For our purposes, I have a problem with the latter. Quitting in this context is not admitting defeat. It's admitting to yourself that you can be happier and have a better life. That is, if you're willing to leave a bad situation behind.

When faced with such decisions, there are many excuses for staying in a bad situation: you may fear that the new workplace won't give you the happiness you crave or that making a move could create new and more challenging problems. Changing jobs is often stressful, but is it worth staying for years in a bad situation that you know makes you unhappy? After doing your due diligence, if the only roadblock is fear of change, you need the courage to make it happen. Often, some vocations are better suited for us at different times in our lives, and quitting is needed to pivot in a better direction. Sometimes, people know quitting will immediately lead to bigger success, but for various reasons.

Take actress Molly Shannon, who quit "Saturday Night Live" at the height of her popularity on the show. Was she unhappy? "No, quite the opposite," Shannon told Howard Stern in 2022. "This is the greatest job I'll ever have in my life, and I still feel that way."

"So, why leave after six years?" Stern replied.

"Because I loved it so much," Shannon said. "I loved (SNL creator and producer) Lorne (Michaels) and respected the show so much, I wanted to leave when I loved it. I've seen some people stay on too long when they're phoning it in, and I was like, 'I gotta hand the torch over.' I had been working so hard. I just wanted to enjoy my life."

Quitting can be the right move for many reasons!

Shannon's example is the outlier, but I see many peers in my business (and I know you can relate) who either stay in a job they hate or get laid off and keep trying to get back into a career that no longer fits them. In my sports media field, the members of the old guard who worked in local news and newspapers for years are consistently being replaced by younger candidates who are either cheaper options or have fresh faces that executives believe look more appealing on camera. Seasoned veterans in my business complain not about where they work but why they aren't given the same opportunities they used to receive. So, they hold on by hosting podcasts or launching websites that are often dead-end solutions. Often, this results in not making nearly the money they have earned for years. Many are close-minded, refusing to utilize talents they have built for decades to pursue other possibilities.

The solution: Find something better using the skill set you have acquired for years.

There is no one simple solution to quitting and pivoting with a plan. There could be many, but it's important for you not to get stuck in a wheel like a hamster, spinning in the same direction yet ignoring the many options that could make you as happy or, in many cases, happier than where you found yourself before you were laid off.

It's one thing to have a passion for something, but we must match our talents with that passion. I love many things I'm not good at: golf, throwing a football, playing the guitar; I'd love to be able to slam dunk a basketball. Learn to know your limits, embrace what you do well, and, most importantly, enjoy doing it.

We all have our talents.

While the guitar option may be realistic, I'll never dunk a basketball, throw a football 60 yards, or consistently shoot rounds of golf in the '70s.

The lesson: Be honest about your skill set and channel your efforts in the right direction for optimum results.

Search for what you are good at—and go for it!

I believed strongly that I would be a good sportscaster, but that wasn't the consensus among my bosses, especially in my early years. In my first job in Tuscaloosa, I was passed over for the main sports anchor job, and then, after getting my second break in Tallahassee, an imperfect storm nearly caused me to leave my passion and settle for a career I would have hated.

I was hired at the number one station in the market, and I was excited about making a move. It was a pivotal time in my life as I was just married, but when I arrived, I immediately saw a disconnect between myself and my superiors. Many have been where I was, feeling good about a newfound opportunity but learning quickly that it isn't the right fit. I wanted to make the best of it, but I soon realized that my current climate's dysfunction wouldn't improve.

Frankly, I stayed at this station for far too long. In the nearly three years

I worked there, I was labeled as someone who wasn't focused, organized, and a renegade of sorts—labels I had never been accused of prior or since. It was a toxic environment. I was even accused of stealing a phone one day! The next day, my accusers found the missing phone but offered me no apology. They passed me over for a promotion, telling me that while I was good on air, I was weak in other areas. Frustration abounded in every direction.

The whole experience affected my confidence, and I seriously questioned if I had a future in the business. I was starting to believe what they were saying, and it was taking its toll on my professional and private life.

Then, a friend and a co-worker sat me down and gave me some advice that stays with me today. It's advice that I have often passed on to others: "Sometimes in life," she said, "some people just don't like you." Simple words and a frank message, but it's true. I was simply a square peg in the round hole of a mid-market TV station. I could stay there, be unhappy, settle for mediocrity, or do something about it.

Think about how many people you have worked with over the years who can't stand their jobs but stay and complain daily about their plight instead of leaving. It makes for a bad workplace, and it's no way to live.

It's OK to quit, but you have to have a plan!

Let me make this clear: I don't like quitting anything. I take great pride in grinding things out, knowing I love what I do but understanding I won't always love where I do it. But there are exceptions to the rule, and this station qualified. My sports director was unstable, and my news director condoned his behavior, worsening the situation. I remember receiving compliments from my news director for a story that had aired, only to have my sports director rip the piece to shreds. Too many mixed messages and no leadership equated to a miserable work experience and after too many months and years, I realized it was time to make my move.

But I had to have a plan!

Shortly after being accused of stealing a phone, I knew I needed to map out my departure. So, I applied for several jobs and put out several feelers. Soon thereafter, a freelance opportunity opened up that would pay me more in a few months than I would make in almost a year at the TV station.

It seemed like a sign.

After another rough weekend, I called my news director to put in my notice. I thought he would be happy to see me go, but he spent an hour convincing me to stay. He explained that we're in a tough business and that quitting would hurt my career, to which I countered, "But why would I stay somewhere where I've been accused of stealing, been passed over for promotions, and been labeled incorrectly?"

He had no answer. He wasn't used to people quitting without another job to go to. That meeting spurred my confidence. I needed to quit, and there were better people to work with who would appreciate what I had to offer. Think about this the next time you are faced with a similar situation.

Don't take yourself and your skills for granted!

So, I put in my two-week notice, and two weeks later, I started working my freelance job. Then, just like that, a competing station called with a job offer to place me in a better position than my previous stop. It was validation of not only trusting my instincts and believing that while some people don't like you, those people don't define you either. I remember my first day at my new place. Knowing I was in a better spot where my work would be appreciated was liberating.

Ten months later, I was hired by a station in an even bigger market, and my salary more than doubled.

So, leaving the station where I was unhappy and underappreciated was the best thing I could have done. I often look back and think how things would have been different if I had stayed. I want to pass on the lesson that you are never out of options, even if you are unsure about your talents. You must believe in yourself and understand that while some may not like you, others will. Surround yourself with those who like you and appreciate what you offer. The result will be greater happiness and, ultimately, better production because you positioned yourself in a better situation.

You need to find those who appreciate you!

The lesson: It's ok to quit, if you have a plan.

Arnold Schwarzenegger's inner circle made his successful pivots possible. Those who believed in him pushed him to leave his home country to find success in the United States. They opened doors for him and helped him improve himself from both a training and communications standpoint. These skills made the pivot from Mr. Universe to the lead role in "The Terminator" possible.

Having the right relationships is vital, but you must possess the self-confidence to push yourself forward to places you may be scared of, which will ultimately take you to places you could never imagine.

For Schwarzenegger, becoming a leading man proved so many wrong, but taking roles in comedy? That was a whole new ballgame.

In the 1980s, director Ivan Reitman was churning out hits. Hit after hit, from Meatballs to Stripes to all the Ghostbusters movies, he was the king of comedy.

While on vacation in Aspen, Colorado, Schwarzenegger randomly bumped into Reitman as both stepped out of one of the area's resorts. Arnold saw Reitman and said, "You that Ghostbuster guy, you know I could be a Ghostbuster."

That led to a dinner with Reitman, during which the respected director was caught off guard by Arnold's personality, speech, and humor. Reitman told Schwarzenegger, "We'll make a move one day together," which he confirmed in the Arnold documentary.

The lesson: Trust your instincts. Schwarzenegger felt confident enough to contact Reitman. Reitman, in turn, felt good enough about the dinner that he would bet on himself and his new friend from Aspen.

That chance meeting around the ski slopes led to a movie no one would have once had the courage to make, let alone a project many would have never pegged as a success just a few years earlier. Let's team up the action hero and former Mr. Universe with one of the world's best comedic stars and label them "Twins."

"Twins," featuring Schwarzenegger and the diminutive Danny DeVito, was a smashing success. It opened as the number-one film in the United States and stayed on top for the next two weekends. It grossed $112 million domestically, making it the fifth biggest-grossing film in the United States in 1988.

In addition, Schwarzenegger and DeVito bet on themselves. Instead of taking their usual salaries for this film, the two co-stars, along with Reitman, agreed with the studio to take collectively 40% of the film's box office and rental returns.

The film grossed $216 million worldwide, which resulted in the trio receiving the biggest paychecks of their film careers.

The successful comedic pivot also ensured the trust of Schwarzenegger with Reitman, who cast him in the highly successful "Kindergarten Cop" two years later. "It was one of those interesting switches that you had to make where something worked for you," Schwarzenegger said in his "Arnold" documentary.

POLITICAL PIVOT

So, the once shy kid from Austria grew confident performing on the big stage as Mr. Universe and Olympian in the bodybuilding world. Schwarzenegger used those skills to study acting and harness his communication skills to become a leading man.

He still wanted more. What was the natural pivot between the bodybuilder and the actor?

Politics???

Before running for governor of California, Schwarzenegger was indoctrinated into the political world by meeting his future wife, Maria Shriver. She was a member of the Kennedy family, which boasted quite a political track record and, ultimately, a strong influence on the current leading man in Hollywood.

As a result, Schwarzenegger became involved nationally with the Special Olympics and was appointed by President George H.W. Bush as Chairman of the President's Council of Physical Fitness in Sports.

Suddenly, serving took precedence over performing. A pivot to politics became Schwarzenegger's new passion. "I realized how much fun this is. I was happier than being on a movie set," he confided in "Arnold."

With his home state of California demanding a recall of unpopular governor Gray Davis, the current actor and former bodybuilder faced a dilemma: could he win the governor's race if he only had a few months to run?

At 56, with plenty of money and a career he enjoyed, he had every reason to say no. However, this unconventional candidate announced most unconventionally, saying he would run for governor on "The Tonight Show with Jay Leno."

Most thought it was a joke at the time, but his inner circle, including James Cameron, believed it. "Who knew he was spending that time preparing for his biggest part?" Cameron said in the documentary.

The pivot to politics saw the critics of Schwarzenegger come full circle. He confided in his documentary, "The very agents and managers and studio executives that said to me in the 70s, 'you will never make it don't ever get into acting' are the very same that said, 'Are you crazy, you're making 20-20 million a movie now.' But the more someone says that you can't or this is impossible, the more I get excited over it."

At his core, Schwarzenegger approached politics like he did acting and bodybuilding. He embraced a new career he was passionate about. He saw his mindset as different from others. He wanted this because, unlike many, he would enjoy it.

"Most people don't know that, they worry and they work and they worry and the work, where's the fun?"

The lesson: Pivoting isn't easy, but if it were, everybody would do it! Find your passion by taking chances.

It was a successful broken record with Schwarzenegger. He found success by using the skills he had acquired to make a successful pivot, this time in pursuit of the governorship of California.

It started with his ability to communicate, a trait he developed as a shy teenage boy in Austria. This trait eventually manifested a legendary career in two arenas and now prepped him for a third.

"I knew that was my strength, to communicate and to penetrate. Not just the brain, but the heart," he said in the documentary.

The skill set Schwarzenegger had perfected in years of performing translated into how he prepped for his political debates. "I did exactly what I did in bodybuilding. I did my training, but I also was thinking about how can I derail (my opponents) psychologically.

"I had my comedy writers write up some jokes. So, whenever I did not know the issues well, I would just use the jokes."

It all worked for Schwarzenegger, who amazingly became the 38th governor in California's history. He won re-election and served for seven years. He left office with a $37 billion infrastructure package, the strictest environmental laws in the state's history, and an impressive track record of diversity regarding women and minority appointments for judges.

For a man who had built quite a career on sequels, it was completing an impressive trilogy of pivots. His transformation from bodybuilder to leading man to the governor was impressive, but like Lisa Kudrow, he needed help from others at every stop.

All successful pivots require quality relationships that tell the truth, build confidence, and provide the courage to make your next move.

Arnold Schwarzenegger takes great pride in his many pivots but doesn't buy that he's a self-made man; he needed help from others at each stop along the way.

"The only thing that is self is kind of my motivation and my visualization and all that stuff. There were endless amounts of people that were helping me, but don't ever call me a self-made man, because I'm not."

A modest statement from a man who rewrote the history books on pivoting.

PIVOTING TO SUCCESS (USING YOUR PREVIOUS SKILLS)

Drew Fellios is a successful play-by-play announcer for ESPN, a notion that seemed far-fetched in his early years. You see, Drew had to overcome a hurdle that would hinder the confidence of anyone who aspired to be a sportscaster. He had a speech impediment.

"When I was growing up, I was a hardcore stutterer," Drew reveals. "As a teenager, I struggled with that. A lot."

Never more so perhaps than one day during his junior year in high school when he was asked to deliver a speech while running for vice president of his school's student body. This future national broadcasting talent was filled with nerves as he addressed a crowd of 600 fellow students.

"I got up to give the speech and the hand I was holding the microphone in began to shake," Fellios remembered. "I absolutely made a complete fool of myself that day. The whole class laughed at me. I'll never forget it, one of the most embarrassing things in my life."

A lot of people would have given up their dreams after suffering such a humiliating experience. They would have quit. Not Drew. He fought on. Instead of quitting, he went to a speech therapist who built Drew's confidence, ridding him of his stutter. Then, a year later, Drew ran for office again. And won!

"Having experienced that humiliating moment made me want to come back and do it again, only better," Drew said.

Drew refused to allow an early obstacle define him as he built on his newfound momentum by pushing new boundaries. He went from struggling through a speech that could have set him back to moving forward and putting himself out there again by reading the class announcements, where he found his voice and passion.

"That's when I thought, 'Wait a minute, I think I can do something with this.'" Drew recalled.

Drew found his voice and his calling simultaneously. He wanted to be a sportscaster. Heading to college, he majored in Communications, worked for the college radio station, and later found work at small television stations in West Virginia, Florida, and Nebraska.

Drew then pivoted for the first time in his career. Mired in small-market television, he took a chance and returned to his hometown of Tampa to work for a startup sports network that concentrated primarily on high school sports. It was an opportunity to hone his broadcast skills as a play-by-play announcer. It was a natural fit, and Drew was soon noticed by ESPN, which hired him to call games nationally, primarily in the sport he loves the most, basketball.

After reaching the pinnacle of his profession, Fellios could have gotten comfortable, but at his core, he knew he wanted more out of life and his career.

"ESPN was my greatest achievement, earning a full-time contract and being one of the main guys they relied on," Drew said. "That was a thrill, I admit, but after you're in it, you realize you can't let it define you."

Fellios had an established track record as a national broadcaster at that point in his life. His talents allowed him to pick up more work, calling games for professional sports teams and networks for various sports, but he wanted more. The turning point was the pandemic and the crushing death of his father, with whom he was very close. These events changed his mindset, and he wanted to see what other options he could explore. For years, Drew was impressed with many of his peers in other careers, such as attorneys, financial advisors, and various CEOs of companies who had created their businesses and voices in different areas. "I dealt with a lot of those people when I was in broadcasting, and I was in awe."

The time was now to pivot in a different sense. Drew didn't let go of his broadcasting duties. He just wanted to add more to his plate. Even though he was successful, Drew felt incomplete, knowing the skill set he had acquired could provide more opportunities.

"Here I am. I've accomplished a lot in broadcasting, but I'm just the man on the microphone," Drew said. "I'm commentating on what's happening but not making it happen. You can only talk about something happening for so long. Eventually, you want to jump in and make something happen yourself."

That something would be his newfound passion for real estate.

While buying his first home, Fellios discovered how hard it is to find someone you can trust, someone who can put the customer at ease. He saw an opening, and after conferring with realtors he respected, Drew took the plunge and pivoted.

"Once everything worked out (with my own home purchase) I realized that there are probably a lot of people out there just like me that are scared about making the biggest purchase of their life and don't know where to start," Drew said.

"So I kind of figured, 'You know what, this is right up my alley. I really want to do this.' I think there is a need out there for people to deal with people they can trust, and that's how I got into selling real estate."

Having the motivation is one thing, but Drew, despite a brief stint selling shoes in college, knew that becoming the seller of big-time properties wouldn't be easy.

"You can imagine how excited I was to sell people $700,000 and $800,000 condos."

Pivoting in his new lane was hardly easy at first. "When you start in real estate, you get humbled because you don't know how to talk the lingo. There was one couple that I probably took on ten different showings, and they didn't have any ambition to buy anything. They were kind of using me because I was new."

Learning the ropes was an adjustment for Fellios, who didn't sell a house for months after getting his license.

"The first few months, there were moments where I was like, 'I don't know if I can do this,'" Drew remembered. "That's when you start to bang your head against the wall. Then, just like in TV, where you click the TV on to see what the other guys are doing, you see the same names up there, and you're wondering, 'How in the heck can I break the mold? How do I get in with these people? How do I do this?' And then you just kind of realize once it happens, one thing leads to another."

Perseverance, hard work, and a belief in his new plan helped Drew thrive in his new passion.

"There were moments where I thought, 'I can't do this, this is over my head, I just need to go back to broadcasting,'" Drew said. "But then, once you start to do it and you see the ball go through the hoop a few times, you realize, 'Ok, this is how it's done.'"

The irony of this sports analogy revealed Drew's newfound dual career. It was successful because Fellios incorporated the skills that made him a successful sportscaster into his transition into real estate. First and foremost, he used his people skills.

"Talking to people is big," Drew acknowledges.

He found the same trust he built in his new passion aligned with those he interviewed as a reporter. This skill transcended his clients, where the commonality was his ability to convey a sincere approach that he was on their side. The art of selling isn't selling. It's becoming an advocate or borrowing another sports analogy, showing that you are on the same team.

"I try to partner with my clients and get them where they need to go," Drew said. "That's my job. The moment I try to sell them on anything, I'm dead."

Fellios worked hard to become a great play-by-play man by gathering stories for his broadcast from players and coaches he built close relationships with. Now, he was transferring those same skills to newfound relationships in the real estate world. Drew's desire to cultivate relationships with his clients was similar to the bonds he developed as a reporter.

"The people that you covered that you grew to love and you saw the work they put in, the high school coaches and some of these families and some of these athletes that never got recognized, you want to partner with them, you want to run through the wall for them," he said.

This is a classic example of pivoting from one passion to another, but Drew's story is slightly different. He held on to one passion while adding another. Sure, his people skills helped, but making this move a success required him to use other skills he had acquired.

"In real estate, just like in sportscasting, you're either out in the field or in your office," Drew said. "You're either out talking to people, shaking hands, and making deals happen, or you're back home looking at the numbers and contracts, planning your next move. That's kind of where it's the same."

Fellios used transferable skills to make his second career work. He also took advantage of something he acquired after being a sportscaster at the local, regional, and national levels: name recognition.

"Getting to the point I have in broadcasting, I think it carries some weight, and whenever another realtor looks you up or tries to figure out, 'Who is this guy?' it doesn't hurt that I've been in broadcasting 25 years and you put my name in google and good things come up," he said.

After selling his first home, Drew gained the confidence and momentum he needed to balance his two different yet similar careers, which keep him busy but provide more balance to his life.

"I'm working a lot, but it's fun," Drew said. "I'm interacting with so many people, and I'm enjoying what I'm doing. I think I'm doing each job better because I'm doing both. If I were just doing one, I'd probably get tired of it, and it would get old, but now I can do both."

TIPS ON PIVOTING SUCCESS?

Fellios has found rare success holding onto his initial passion while adding to his workload through a brand-new career, but what would his advice be for those looking to do the same?

"Be flexible, don't lock yourself in," he said. "Don't think that the company always has your back. You've got to have your back. You have to look at your life and you've got to make those decisions and those choices."

"The other thing is always to look ahead. It's the one thing I've done fairly well in my life. I've made a lot of mistakes, but I have looked ahead to the next ten years, to what's next. I think that if you're in a set job, ten years is a good run. If you're halfway into it or tired of it, you're probably due for a change."

Drew's self-evaluation served him well in looking ahead and being self-aware enough to know when to make a change and which change was right for him.

"Time off is the greatest thing that can happen because it makes you think," he said. "Not too much time off, but it recharges you when you have time off, and you come back better than ever before if you're always riding."

"I've seen so many talented broadcasters, they just kept on doing the same thing, and they never got where they want to be, and they're really good, but they just don't see the forest behind the trees."

This problem is not for just sportscasters facing a fork in the road. It applies to all walks of life. If you feel stuck in your career, you are never out of options. You have to have the gumption, like Drew did, to create more opportunities.

At last check, Drew was among his team's top home sellers. The power of pivoting wins again!

CHAPTER FIVE

IT ONLY TAKES ONE TO LOVE YOU, SO DON'T BE AFRAID TO ASK!

"If you don't ask, the answer is always no. If you don't step forward, you're always in the same place."
Nora Roberts

One of my favorite movies is the romantic comedy, "Say Anything," from which one line personifies the lesson in this chapter. In the movie, the protagonists are two high school seniors: the lovable yet awkward Lloyd Dobler, played by John Cusack, and the beautiful valedictorian of the class, Diane Court, played by Ione Skye. They were the ultimate odd couple, but they defined the adage as "opposites attract." In the movie, one of Diane's classmates asks her why she went on a date with Lloyd?

Her response ... "He asked me?"

Exactly!

It's amazing how often I've succeeded or seen others succeed simply by asking for help, a favor, or, in Lloyd Dobler's case, asking the best-looking girl in school out on a date.

I firmly believe in the old cliche, "You make your luck." Hard work creates opportunities, but new opportunities are often the result of simply asking for permission.

Permission from someone to participate in a project. Permission from a co-worker for help in an area you're either new to or perceive as a weakness. In all cases, asking for permission allows you to grow or improve whatever you are working on.

Often, we are too scared to ask. There are many reasons for that. What if the answer is no? Maybe I'll be embarrassed or look stupid. Pride often gets in the way of progress. But asking can open avenues you never knew existed and turn your outlook into a broader land of opportunities.

Sometimes, all you have to do is ... ask?

For me, the art of asking was in the genes.

It all started in my early years. Again, I credit my Dad for the aggressive nature he instilled in me early on in life.

My desire to go after what I wanted originated from our mutual love of baseball.

Growing up in Florida in the 80s, we had no major league baseball teams. The closest big-league city to us then was Atlanta, home of those Braves, a five-hour drive from my hometown. But we loved baseball so much that we would pick out a series each summer and head north for our baseball fix. On these trips, my Dad had an enterprising idea to research where the opposing team was staying, and we would make that our hotel, thinking we would be in the ideal spot to get autographs.

It was a winning formula, as it's all about location in life. Being in the right position to get the players' autographs at the hotel was an opportunity to connect with them early in the day before droves of fans at the ballpark inundated them with requests. I could get them in the hotel lobby as they waited for the team bus, and sometimes, if I was adventurous, even as they were waiting for a table or in line to check out. I never thought about it until I became a parent, but my Dad must have gotten a kick out of sitting back and watching me hustle for autographs.

That process also taught me the art of asking. Whether it's a teacher, a future boss, a co-worker, or a big-league baseball player, you'll never know the outcome if you don't ask. I remember the excitement of getting players' autographs in ways others wouldn't try. I didn't realize it at the time, but these experiences at a rudimentary level helped prepare me for my future career.

Decades later, in my first job as a sportscaster, I was back in—of all places—Atlanta, covering the National League Championship Series. The Braves were playing the Pittsburgh Pirates, led then by the irritable and often antagonistic Barry Bonds. He wasn't a fan of the media, and many established journalists knew better than to ask Bonds for anything, especially during his pregame routine.

At the time, I didn't know any better, or maybe I felt I had nothing to lose.

I worked for one of the smallest media outlets in the country, a local TV station in Tuscaloosa, Alabama, and there I was, covering a sporting event of this magnitude for the first time. It was intimidating, exhilarating, and an out-of-body experience. Yet, I remember thinking, this is exactly why I wanted to be a sportscaster covering events like this alongside the best reporters in the country.

I remember watching Bonds take batting practice. He was focused, and everyone around him left him alone. He wasn't socializing much with his teammates, much less the media. On this day, with national reporters all around me, nobody approached Bonds, so I figured it was a rare opening, where I could take advantage of the situation.

My videographer looked at me like I was crazy when I suggested we try to get him. I can only imagine his thoughts watching me walk up to Bonds while he was warming up and with so many of our peers watching. It may have been akin to seeing a fawn slowly walking across the street despite the risk of several oncoming cars.

Don't be afraid to ask!

I said, "Barry, could I have a few minutes of your time?" Although it seemed like an hour, Bonds looked at me for a second, took a few practice swings, and finally replied, "Shoot."

The king of media disdain had officially served up the green light.

I asked Bonds three questions. He gave me three decent answers, and then suddenly, the rest of the media contingent invaded my personal Barry Bonds party. I looked around and saw several national reporters I had looked up to for years, suddenly following my lead. I was proud I had put myself out there and survived what could have been a fatal career move.

Just ask!

What is the worst thing that can happen? Someone says no. There are worse things in the world.

Several years later, while working in Jacksonville, I covered a joint practice between the Jacksonville Jaguars and Miami Dolphins. We were under a deadline and covering the Dolphins practice, which had just ended without a press conference, yet I needed a reaction for our six o'clock sportscast. The Dolphins coach at the time was Hall of Famer Jimmy Johnson, who was walking toward the team bus by himself with several players and coaching staff already on board. I approached Jimmy and asked him if I could get a few questions? At first, he ignored me, so I got closer, stuck one foot into the bus, and asked him again. This time, he stopped, turned around, paused, and said, "You can have one question."

I asked him one question, and he gave me an answer good enough to fill the hole I needed in my report. I looked at him, knowing that was it, and said thanks. Johnson then turned and grabbed his seat at the head of the bus.

Mission accomplished! You have to ask. You never know what can happen!

Trust me. You don't always get the desired results. I have been shut down several times, but even in those circumstances, I knew it was better to ask than not try. The takeaway: explore all your options before moving on to your second plan of attack. Don't ever walk away from a situation thinking you could have attained better results just by asking.

The art of asking changed the direction of my young broadcasting career as a weekend anchor in Tallahassee. I felt that to advance, I would have to mix things up. I referenced my "Naborhood" weekly show airing every Sunday night where I would invite a guest each week. This guest wouldn't just be someone I interviewed, but would help me deliver the sportscast. It became an instant hit, and I learned through asking that most players and coaches were happy to be a part of something new.

Just ask!

I have long believed that many grow tired of repeatedly answering the same question, no matter the profession or situation. They crave a new angle or a new platform to participate in. This is why social media has taken on a life of its own. Now, everyone has an online platform to communicate their respective messages. But even with all the technological advances, I still believe that if you build it, they will come, especially if it's something they haven't seen before.

"The Naborhood" show allowed local personalities to be themselves, read the sports report on the teleprompter, and do the highlights of games they didn't participate in. It showed their fans a different side of the athletes' and coaches' personalities. It was a valuable lesson about the importance of asking and, in this case, asking several sports figures to step out of their comfort zones. Not everyone will buy in, but you will be surprised how often people crave to participate in something different and escape the mundane.

I carried that mindset decades later into my job as a college professor, where I was allowed to launch a new sports-related curriculum—not in the communications school but in the school of business. I created courses centered around sports innovation, entrepreneurship, marketing, management, and media concentrations.

In the process, I asked several contacts I've developed over the years, including media peers, athletes, coaches, and team executives, to appear as guest speakers. The amazing part of this asking exercise is over time, most of my guests were those I hadn't previously known; I randomly reached out to many who accepted. Frankly, I still get a kick out of reaching out to those I've never met and gauging their interest. More often than not, I have found that people are willing to give their time, whether it's Barry Bonds before a playoff game, Jimmy Johnson before a Monday Night football game, or some other high-profile sports professional asked to spend an hour talking to my students.

All you have to do is ask!

Whether you're a reporter, an engineer, a lawyer, a doctor, a cosmetologist, or a CEO—asking is more rewarding than not. A Forbes article titled "Need Help? Don't Be Afraid to Ask" revealed that the 'strategic ask' "is critical to solving problems, cultivating breakthroughs, bridging organizational silos, sharing knowledge, and all the other things associated with high-performing teams."

Making a move to ask is a winning formula for success, as highlighted by Dr. Wayne Baker, Director of the Center for Positive Organizations at the University of Michigan, who wrote a book titled, "All You Have to Do Is Ask: How to Master the Most Important Skill for Success." Dr. Baker believes giving and receiving are equally critical keys to success. He contends that the primary hurdle standing between many people and the success they want is a lack of skill in *asking* for what they need.

Baker's book explains how asking involves many layers. Getting through them can increase your productivity at work, improve team chemistry, and ultimately build confidence among your employees. Baker stresses, "In the workplace, asking for help can mean the difference between success and failure."

Think about what you do for a living. You want to impress your boss and co-workers, and while it's important to show initiative, holding back and not asking because you are scared builds up anxiety and frustration. Martin emphasizes, "You never know what people know or who they know until you ask."

A Harvard Study, titled "Smart People, ask for (my) Advice: Seeking Advice Boosts Perceptions of Confidence," concluded that many are reluctant to seek the advice of others out of fear of being incompetent. Yet this fear is misplaced. Ironically, this study found that individuals perceive those who ask for advice to be more competent than those who don't, and this perception is highlighted when the task is difficult.

Baker told Forbes that in this process, some obstacles come into play when we are afraid to ask? "One is that we fear others will think we are incompetent, weak, or can't do our jobs." But research shows that, as long as you make a thoughtful request, people will think you are *more* competent, not less.

PASSION CHASER

Fear plays a big part in asking and pivoting to your new passion. Overcoming those fears has been the modus operandi for one of the most unique performers in the world. Tony Hawk is the best-known skateboarder on the planet. However, his rise to the top of the profession featured many of the tenets highlighted in this book. He is constantly pushing the boundaries and doing feats he's scared of. Like Dave Grohl, Hawk has made millions by following his passion. He loved his craft so much that he would be skateboarding even if it hadn't earned him such unexpected fortune and fame.

In the HBO documentary on Hawk's career, "Until the Wheels Fall Off," the ultimate outlier showed that his initial motivations weren't money or fame. Hawk has remarkably sustained the thrill of his craft for decades. He has just loved skateboarding, not everything that would eventually come with it, "I never got into skateboarding to be famous," he said. I never thought I would be famous."

The GOAT (Greatest of All Time) Skateboarder found his passion early. Initially, the highly competitive Hawk was unsuccessful in traditional sports, admitting in his documentary, "I couldn't do physical things my peers could do. They were bigger and stronger." His early athletic struggles left him so frustrated that his parents had him tested. The results revealed that Hawk had a high IQ, and he was encouraged to take gifted courses. The test also showed that Hawk had an aptitude for skateboarding, a sport in which he soon became a prodigy, turning pro at 14 before making enough money to buy a house by the time he finished his senior year in high school.

Now, while still skating regularly in his mid-50s, Hawk continues to push new boundaries. This despite piling up so many injuries over the years that if you jotted them all down, it would look longer than most grocery lists. But that long list, which includes several concussions, a fractured skull, a battered back, several missing teeth, and a broken thumb and pelvis, is simply a testament to Hawk's fortitude.

And despite the pain, Hawk never imagined doing anything else with his life. "I found this thing I loved more than anything else I've tried or done in my life," Hawk said in the documentary. "I found my purpose and my salvation, and in some ways, I found my emotional highs."

Hawk has tested the boundaries of his sport, as his signature high-flying maneuvers mirrored the sport's up-and-down waves of popularity. Surviving the highs and lows challenged his physical and mental resolve. In the early 90s, the sport was on life support. In a way, so was Hawk. With skate parks closing nationwide, Hawk struggled to find the financial means necessary to provide for his family. At one point, he was so financially strapped he couldn't pay his water bill. Then, questions began to arise from those within his inner circle. Hawk recalled an insider saying, "He's still trying to skateboard. Are you serious?"

At his lowest point, however, Hawk's passion became his remedy.

"I would skate," Hawk said in "Until the Wheels Fall Off." "That's been my escape always. I never considered quitting skating as an option. I was always gonna find time to skate."

And succeed. In the late 90s, as insiders were questioning his undying commitment to skating, Hawk realized his biggest success following the advent of the X Games, which helped turn skateboarding into a mainstream sport. With its new acceptance, Hawk's fame reached new heights as he was made the frontman for a video game dynasty, "Tony Hawk's Pro Skater." The series debuted in 1999 and quickly took off. Since then, it has erupted into 18 different versions, including 10 main-series titles, four spinoffs, and four repackages. This all equated to Hawk receiving many million-dollar checks and elevated him to a new level of fame.

The fame and fortune are great, but Hawk acknowledged in his documentary that the biggest benefit is that all of the success enabled him to prolong his life-long passion, even when it presented painful moments.

"If you're convinced you will fail, that will come to fruition," he said. "I was willing to get hurt along the way, but I didn't visualize myself getting hurt along the way."

For Hawk, there was no other option. Pursuing his love of skateboarding was his only avenue.

"I always approached it like, this was going to work, I'm going to figure this out," he said. "I'm willing to struggle through the learning process, even change my approach, just to figure out how to do it."

The proof of his never-ending passion pursuit was Hawk's crowning moment as a skateboarder. No skater had ever been able to land a 900, which was getting airborne for 2.5 spins. At 31, while competing in the 1999 X-games, his effort symbolized his legendary career, during which he never gave up.

Going past regulation time, Hawk took over the ESPN airwaves with the laser focus that had made him the king of the mountain in his sport. Though it took him 10 tries, Hawk knew he was on the cusp of something special, and finally landed a clean 900 dramatically on network television and in front of a fired-up X-Games audience.

The signature feat only added to Tony Hawk's legend and gave his fans another glimpse into the stubborn, yet steady, drive he had to be the best. That drive has delivered him through a myriad of injuries, several unbelievable highs, and crushing lows. The trend continues as Hawk continues even today to push the boundaries in a sport that many believe to be a young man's game.

"I'm still trying to push the limits," he said. "I don't know how long this will last, but I'm not going to quit."

Not quitting, overcoming his fears, and always "asking" for more challenges. It's no wonder Tony Hawk has reached the top of the skateboarding mountain. The passion has carried him over the ups and downs for decades.

CHAPTER SIX

CATS ARE COOL

"I think you know what you're supposed to do deep down inside, I think everybody does. A lot of people just don't go after it."
Eddie Murphy

He was supposed to be a star.
Not a movie star, a football star.
Ironically, the twists and turns of his life led him to the former, not the latter.
Yet, when his football career ended prematurely, Dwayne Johnson only had seven bucks.
Before he became the iconic "Rock" in wrestling and captivated audiences as a versatile leading man, Johnson could have only imagined how a string of potent pivots would change his life and make him one of the most versatile performers we've ever seen.
"I always say me playing in the NFL wound up being the best thing that never happened to me because it really shaped and informed who I am," Johnson told "The Pivot Podcast."

Dwayne Johnson grew up in California with one passion: football. His goal was to make it to the NFL, and he was on his way with a football scholarship to the University of Miami, where he won a National Championship with the Hurricanes in 1991.

But he was always a backup. Johnson was never an All-American and rarely a starter. He had one start in 39 games and went undrafted after recording 4.5 sacks and 77 tackles in his four seasons in Miami.

Johnson went undrafted and was subsequently cut from the Canadian Football League's (CFL) Calgary Stampeders with the aforementioned seven bucks in his pocket.

For years, University of Miami coaches had encouraged Johnson that he was on track for NFL greatness, but a shoulder injury, coupled with being on a roster littered with several future Hall of Fame players, prevented him from realizing his initial dream.

"The tidal wave of disappointment out of that, that was a rough one for me."

Once his football dream ended, Johnson returned home and lived with his parents in Tampa, having no idea what his future would hold.

His family business was wrestling; Johnson's grandfather and father had wrestled professionally. But like Schwarzenegger, despite not receiving support from his family to make this his career, he pursued it anyway.

Once Johnson pivoted from football to wrestling, he took to it immediately. "First day of training, I was in love, that was it. So in a way, wrestling did save my life," Johnson told, ironically, "The Pivot" podcast hosted by former NFL players Ryan Clark, Fred Taylor and Channing Crowder.

Passion fueled Johnson's pivot, not money. His first wrestling paycheck was 40 dollars. He earned additional revenue taking Polaroid pictures with fans, which included five dollars for a picture and 10 dollars for an autographed photo.

Failing wasn't an option. Sure, Johnson's family had a wrestling background, but it wasn't sustainable. He told "The Pivot" podcast that his family's eventual financial struggles, coupled with his instant attraction to wrestling, were the fuel he needed to find love in his second attempt at making a career in professional sports.

"My goal was just to not be broke, and I used to tell myself this all the time. I used to tell myself specifically, "I cannot be fucking broke."

Johnson has witnessed his family struggle month to month while owning a cleaning company, where it was difficult to pay the bills. "I saw what the end of the road was, and that was being evicted and not having any money".

Dwayne Johnson was self-motivated to make his professional pivot work. "For me, it was I cannot be broke. I don't want that for my family. I also think not being drafted, not being picked up, never getting that call from the league put a chip on my shoulder."

The chip served him well and propelled Johnson into superstardom seemingly overnight. In 1996, after being cut by Calgary in the CFL and dipping his toes into the pro wrestling waters, he immediately put everything into his new endeavor. Not wanting to struggle like his family was his motivation. Still, he paid homage to his father and grandfather and initially picked a stage name in Rocky Maivia, combining both of their previous wrestling names. His father wrestled professionally as Rocky Johnson, while his grandfather was High Chief Peter Maivia.

Rocky Maivia didn't last long, nor did Dwayne's anonymity in the wrestling world. A year after coming on the scene representing his family, he quickly made a name for himself as one of the entertaining wrestlers, now known as, "The Rock."

This reinvention saw "The Rock" take hold of the WWF, and later the WWE, and become one of the sport's biggest stars from 1997 to 2004. Johnson's character would become legendary in wrestling circles, along with Hulk Hogan, Ric Flair, and John Cena.

But the legend would grow, as "The Rock" would pivot into acting in 2004.

When I pivoted from being a sportscaster to creating my own company, the year was 2009. Social media was in its infantile stage, and we had no idea how technology would impact our daily lives. Back then, I built my multimedia marketing company brick by brick or, rather, call by call. Yes, I picked up an old-fashioned telephone and had real conversations with many potential clients.

What a concept, right?

Know what I discovered? That most people are willing to hear what you have to say.

I know what you're thinking; that was effective in 2009, but that won't be the case in today's tech-savvy era.

I disagree. I still have success picking up the phone, and more often than not, those on the other end of the line are happy to give me a few minutes to hear why I think they would be a great client.

I'm not alone. Hall of Fame quarterback Peyton Manning enjoys communicating the old-fashioned way, too. Ever the old soul, Manning is known for using another artifact: the old handwritten letter. Peyton has routinely written letters to players who have just retired, coaches he respects, and fans. Talking to Los Angeles Times writer Sam Farmer, Manning credits his family for passing on such an old-school tradition.

"My mother sent me an article one day on the fact that the handwritten letter was becoming a lost art in the text-messaging and email world," Manning told Farmer. "My mother writes handwritten letters. So, I've got to give credit to her."

Several have felt the sincere and unique impact of Manning's letters, including Hall of Fame safety John Lynch, who told Farmer how much it meant to receive one of Peyton's signature hand-written gestures upon retirement.

"I was so touched that the first letter I got when I retired was from Peyton," Lynch said. "It was a handwritten note that meant more than the gift. He sent a case full of Silver Oak wine."

Speaking of alcohol, Manning's business pursuit, in which he started his line of bourbon, didn't call for any letters. Cold calls did the trick just fine. Manning told Indianapolis Star reporter Dana Hunsinger Benbow that calling potential vendors around the Hoosier state was something he made a priority before launching his Sweetens Cove Tennessee Bourbon. Manning found that picking up a phone and calling many Indiana liquor stores was an effective game plan. His approach during those calls was practiced and executed just like plays from the playbook he worked from during his playing days. For every call, Manning had a rehearsed approach at the ready:

"Um. Hey, this is Peyton Manning. I've got a really good liquor brand called Sweetens Cove. It's got the craziest story behind its name, you know. It's smooth, and I think your customers might like it. Would you be interested in, um, trying it out?"

Manning had the sales pitch down but faced a unique obstacle: He was too famous. The former quarterback discovered some outlets didn't believe it was him and thought it was a prank call. This is further proof that the cold call is effective. People aren't receiving calls as much as they used to, especially from a business owner with the cache of Peyton Manning. The efforts paid off, though.

"I do at least kind of get a response and call back," Manning told the Indianapolis Star. "But the bourbon has to do it after that. It has to be good."

That's a great point Manning makes. I can say that from experience. When I started my company in 2009, I learned you could market your business all you want, but eventually, your product must have staying power. I remember delivering an introductory presentation to one of my first clients, The Humane Society of Tampa Bay. I was prepared and polished, and I knew what to deliver to this organization. After meeting with them and feeling I had nailed the presentation, I was anxious to hear their feedback. Then the CEO said, "This all sounds great, but you better be good." That motivated me.

How did I get the Humane Society as a client? Via a cold call. Earlier in this book, I mentioned how my business pivoted from sports to nonprofits after a chance meeting on a flight where I landed a client for whom we produced a PSA. That gave me the confidence to pursue similar clients, knowing we could bring them similar successes. I aimed to land at least "five" solid leads daily via a cold call.

What is a solid lead? It's a contact I would have a chance to meet with, one I viewed as a viable potential client who could benefit from our services. Every day, I would target select nonprofits and local businesses similar to those we had already succeeded in helping, new businesses in need of promotion, or established businesses that needed a new message.

I never liked sending a blanket email because people get hundreds of them weekly!

I think it's important to at least try a cold call as an introduction to set up a meeting or leave a voicemail and follow up with an email. This can help separate you from the pack because most people appreciate someone who goes the extra mile. Now, you must understand that some don't want you to call. But I found that most people had time to talk or at least say, "Thanks, but we already have a similar service." Either way, it's worth making the cold call to start the conversation because it gives you a better chance to launch a meaningful relationship.

Over the years, I acquired clients in several ways, including meeting them in random places like the airport. I landed a huge organization at one of my daughter's birthday parties. I also picked up clients through referrals, but my number one hook for growing my business was researching the best connection and making the first move via a cold call. It worked when I started the company at the dawn of social media and before the avalanche of technology, and it still rings true today. My cold calls allowed me to pick up clients in all areas of the nonprofit world, including the Humane Society, organizations centered around combating drug addiction, childcare-centric organizations, government entities, and many more. After several years of building my business in this fashion, I improved the delivery of my message, making it more succinct and powerful. As a result, my cold call techniques became more effective. I also learned to follow up those calls with better emails that included samples of our work. I then graduated to communicate through attention-grabbing e-blasts with different themes. But it all started with the cold call.

Most people don't cold call anymore. Don't be most people!

My relationship with the Humane Society afforded me one of my best cold-call success stories. After my "you better be good" meeting with the executive hierarchy, I left respecting this organization even more and wanted to make them proud to have partnered with us. One of my selling points was my relationship with Tampa Bay area sports teams. I was confident I could bring them together with the Tampa Bay Lightning,

Bucs, and Rays, and in time, we did just that.

The first project the Humane Society wanted us to produce was a PSA promoting cat adoptions. The research shows dogs are easier to find homes for, so they wanted me to seek out a sports personality to front a promotion on finding more homes for cats. I had worked for the Lightning in the past and frankly found hockey players to be among the most accessible athletes in all of sports. So, I made a few cold calls to see what I could get. While Tampa Bay's NHL team was helpful, there was bad news: none of their players or coaches had an affinity for cats. So, it was on to Plan B.

I was hopeful the Tampa Bay Rays would be the answer as they were led at the time by one of the most accessible managers in the big leagues, Joe Maddon. Unfortunately, there were a lot of dog lovers in the Rays clubhouse, but neither Maddon nor anyone on his team was a cat lover. At the bottom of the ninth, we rallied as the savior was the Rays mascot, a larger-than-life cat, the infamous DJ Kitty. The team agreed to have DJ Kitty front the PSA. I had the Humane Society, its workers, several volunteers, and approximately 30 cats come to the Rays' home, Tropicana Field, for this unconventional shoot.

For this campaign, I developed the theme "Cats are Cool," which the organization would use on T-shirts. It was our tagline with DJ Kitty and his newfound entourage. It was also the breakthrough I needed to foster a trusted relationship with the Humane Society and the catalyst for our team's great work moving forward.

It was all the result of a cold call!

From there, we were off and running, as the Humane Society wanted my company to produce a PSA to break down the often-negative stereotypes associated with pit bulls. The message: Not all pit bulls are violent. The perfect analogy, I thought, was hockey players. For many, the sport of hockey conjures images of gruesome fights, but as I mentioned earlier, hockey players are among the best pro athletes to deal with because they're generally the most congenial. So when I revisited the Lightning to propose this project, I got the approval of one of their best players, defenseman Victor Hedman, a dog lover who was happy to front the PSA.

Hedman gave us an all-star caliber performance just as he does on the ice. Following a practice one day, we brought a pit bull named Wily, and Hedman immediately embraced him. He skated with him and introduced him to some of his teammates, including the team's best player, Steven Stamkos, who agreed to make a quick cameo.

Hedman was so cooperative he let us put peanut butter on his face so that Wily could lick it off him, which made for a better video. The theme of this project was "Tough Guys need love too," and it was another big success. What made it even more successful was that it sparked a longstanding relationship between the Humane Society and the Tampa Bay Lightning, which joined forces for a yearly calendar and several ticket giveaways and events at their facility geared around Hedman. The organization was touched when a few days after the shoot Hedman called to check in on Wily to see if he had found a home. Hedman ultimately adopted a dog from the organization a few weeks after our shoot.

This all happened because of one impactful cold call!

The success of the Lightning and Rays shoots inspired more work, as our next target was a partnership with the Tampa Bay Buccaneers. The goal for this PSA wasn't cats or pit bulls, but the Humane Society's challenge of finding homes for big dogs. To make this work, we needed a large football player. Working with the Bucs, we found what was then the team's best defensive player, Gerald McCoy, a 6-foot-4, 300-pound defensive lineman. McCoy checked all the boxes. He's big, eloquent, fun-loving, and a pet lover. There was just one problem. He didn't own a big dog. McCoy showed up for the shoot with his tiny Shih Tzu.

Our script was centered around big dogs, but the change-up McCoy threw us provided the opportunity to add a light moment to the project. The shoot went well as McCoy nailed his takes and had fun tossing tennis balls and running around the practice fields with the big dogs. We wrapped up the PSA with McCoy's holding his little Shih Tzu and saying, "But don't forget about the small fries either." It was a win-win. After the shoot, the Humane Society was happy, the Bucs were happy, and McCoy was happy. Knowing that, despite the obstacles, I had brought this respected organization together with all three Tampa Bay sports teams was a rewarding feeling. It gave the organization credibility, and it gave me a wealth of confidence that I could do much more with my company in the coming years.

All due to the magic of a single cold call!

Cold calls have given me a powerful tool to pivot within my passion. They took my business to heights that merely sending emails never would have. We live in an age of short attention spans and ultra-techie times, but sometimes it's okay to kick it old school. Pick up a phone—trust me, it still works.

PIVOTING TO NEW HEIGHTS

It seems Dwayne Johnson's calling was wrestling, but he wanted more. Like Arnold Schwarzenegger, he saw himself building on his initial career and becoming an actor.

Johnson's pivot from wrestling to Hollywood happened much quicker, even though his beginning in the entertainment world mirrored Schwarzenegger's. While Arnold gained traction as an actor playing a bodybuilder, Johnson found his first roles were basically playing himself in music videos and sitcoms. "The Rock" played a wrestler in popular shows such as "Star Trek" and "That '70s Show" before moving to full-blown action hero.

He immediately succeeded in that role, and his motion picture debut saw Johnson portraying "The Scorpion King" in the 2001 movie, "The Mummy Returns." Amazingly, the movie broke a two-year record for the highest-grossing single day in film history, earning over 28 million dollars. His debut earned him a quick single and promotion, and in 2002, he had the leading role in the movie's sequel, "The Scorpion King." Guinness World Records named Johnson the record-holder for the highest-paid actor in their first leading role, where he earned 5.5 million.

His success was further proof that if you find something you love, often you will succeed, and just as often, the money will come. "I'm pretty good at those things that I love to do," Johnson told "The Pivot" podcast. "I like to say whatever that thing is, I run towards it."

His passion would lead Johnson, like Schwarzenegger, to pivot to places his critics never thought he would conquer. "The Rock" would pivot from action roles to becoming a versatile performer, starring as an agent in "Get Smart," a cab driver in "Race to Witch Mountain," and, wait for it, a hockey player turned "Tooth Fairy" in a Disney film with the same name.

Dwayne Johnson's moves were guided by the desire not to fail and not to go broke, but they all worked because he followed careers he was passionate about.

"I get up in the morning and I think about it," he says to "The Pivot" podcast hosts while getting animated and clapping his hands. "I'm gonna run towards the thing, there's a shot I can be pretty good at it. I'd say I'm pretty good at the stuff I love."

The love ensured Johnson would succeed despite leaving his first love, the game of football, with only seven bucks.

Seven turned into quite the lucky number for Dwayne Johnson, who, in 2012, pivoted again, this time by starting his own production company. There, he would oversee projects he may star in but pivot to being an executive producer for many, too.

What was the name of this company?

How about "Seven Bucks Productions."

The memory and the motivation of those impactful seven bucks propelled Dwayne to heights he could never have imagined decades prior.

"I am gonna scratch and claw and kick and bite my way to have more than seven bucks," he told "The Pivot" podcast hosts.

These days Johnson is worth much more than his impactful seven bucks. Since pivoting from his legendary wrestling career, his films have grossed over $10.5 billion worldwide, making him one of the world's highest-paid actors.

Dwayne Johnson could have stopped wresting or acting but pivoted into the business world and found similar passions and, ultimately, success. He is the founder of Teremana Tequila, valued at around $3.5 billion. He is the co-owner of the United Football League (UFL), a professional American football league designed to aid players like the young Johnson—still pursuing their football dreams.

He's on the board of directors of TKO Group Holdings, the parent company of UFC and WWE, proof that he is still consumed by everything that has been a part of his journey: wrestling, football, and now movies. His entertainment production company, Seven Bucks Productions, continues to evolve and adapt, just like its founder.

Johnson never lost the chip on his shoulder and refused to stop pivoting towards his passion, getting hungrier every step of his amazing journey.

What is the secret to Dwayne Johnson's fearless fight to the top? He never let his foot off the gas, even though he had repeatedly found success at every pivot. He never had the mindset that ... he made it.

"Because to me, I'm a couple of days away from (the mindset of) being broke, or we're going to get kicked out (referring to fears his family had of getting evicted). It's like I've never arrived," Johnson told "The Pivot" podcast.

"It was never, I wanna make millions. It was, I need more than seven bucks."

CHAPTER SEVEN

"RUNNING ERRANDS"

"The only source of knowledge is experience. You need experience to gain wisdom."
Albert Einstein

Y ou don't have to dislike your job to pivot; often, you just need to trust your newfound passion. I'm sure many of you have hobbies that you see as having the potential to become a side hustle.

Many people struggle with the dilemma of whether it is sustainable to leave a stable job for something they could find more passion in.

Leslie Frelow had such a job as senior director at the Universal Service Administrative Company, a nonprofit organization under the Federal Communications Commission (FCC) in Washington, D.C.

Frelow enjoyed her job but also enjoyed her hobby of leading virtual wine tastings and tours to Maryland Wineries, a side business she saw great potential in after reading a story chronicled by CNBC.com writer Morgan Smith.

The potential for Frelow's endeavor included an untapped market in the wine industry: supporting sommeliers, farmers, and winemakers of color. According to the Association of African American Vintners, less than 1% of U.S. wineries are black-owned.

Frelow attempted her pivot by launching "The Wine Concierge," an online wine store and subscription wine club. She left behind a stable full-time job to pursue her passion and has found success.

Like any business owner, the challenges she encountered while venturing out into a market with unfavorable demographics wasn't easy, but the freedom of creating her lane has paid off. "It's given me the ultimate flexibility to be there for my aging parents and to pursue something I really love, which is seeing people's excitement from trying wines they didn't know existed," Frelow told CNBC.com.

Pivoting is rarely easy, but Frelow contends she wouldn't trade being an entrepreneur "for anything."

PIVOTING "BACK TO" MY PASSION

My experience in pivoting has been rewarding but hardly easy. When I started my company, seeing all the newfound control I had in my life was fulfilling, but with it came new pressures. No, I no longer had to worry about sports networks cutting budgets and affecting my future, but the importance of bringing in business now fell on my lap. This was both challenging and liberating. When I took matters into my own hands, it was nice that the burden fell on me; it motivated me to succeed more than ever, but it wasn't always smooth sailing. With those new responsibilities came many obstacles.

After my company landed its first nonprofit client, which gave us a lot of work, I thought, 'If only I could have 10 clients like this, I would be a huge success.' The funny thing about business is that after I acquired 10 clients like my first, I lost that initial client! And through no fault of my own. I found that one of the biggest challenges you face in starting a business is clearing obstacles that you have no control over. For example, when the hierarchy of a particular organization changes, the value the new leadership puts on your services can change.

The lesson: Never assume you have a client for life. Always work like nothing is guaranteed.

When I lost my first client, it was due to an abrupt departure of the old guard, the executives who had brought me in and valued our work. Over the years, I had built a strong working relationship with that organization's CEO, VP, and Communications Director. When they left for a variety of reasons, as a result, I soon followed. The new regime didn't see value in our services like the previous one did. It was a powerful lesson, a reminder never to grow complacent.

After years of success with nonprofits, I saw a shift in trends, an impactful change that forced me to pivot in new directions. What I realized was that we were being turned down for three reasons:

- Our prospective clients couldn't afford us.
- Amid developments in technology, organizations knew they could hire younger employees to do the same work, albeit less polished, for less.
- Or they would hire larger companies that donate their services on an in-kind basis. Often, they would write off their services and provide the same work we would have.

These scenarios played out in different forms and fashions for a few years before I realized we had to pivot to survive. In situations like this, it's vital for an entrepreneur to be self-aware and try to rectify a problem before it begins to eat away at the core of their business. In our case, we still had several nonprofit clients. But I knew that if we didn't start pivoting, we would be in trouble.

After examining the current economy's landscape and our company's strengths and weaknesses, I thought it was in our best interests to go back to our roots and do what we did best, what we knew best: sports.

Although I had found success by pivoting away from sports, I remained an active sportscaster because the craft of storytelling will always be at my core. So, when the nonprofit side of my business model began to change, I thought of ways to make back the money via sports.

Out of nowhere, an idea came to me that soon became an obsession, and I was determined to develop. I had seen the success of CBS' late-night talk show host James Corden's carpool karaoke segments, where he drives around with select musicians and sings their most popular songs. I was also impressed with Jerry Seinfeld's successful Netflix series, "Comedians in Cars Getting Coffee," where he went down memory lane with various funny men and women on how they approached their routines. Both were great ideas.

I aimed to create a similar series, gear it around sports, and make it different from Corden and Seinfeld's ideas. I also wanted to create an opportunity to sit down with athletes and sports personalities in a more personal setting. Modern technology has widened the gap between athletes and the media, and I wanted to close that gap a bit.

The answer was a concept I called "Errands." My audience and I would get to know sports celebrities better by simply running errands with them. Everyone runs errands, right? Of course, they do. This series would humanize athletes by showing them doing something we all do.

My plan was to select sports personalities of all kinds. While they ran three errands of their choice, I would tag along and carry on meaningful conversations with them about their lives, their successes, their failures, and what it was that made them tick.

My idea revolved around a lost art in this social media age: getting to know people one-on-one and developing relationships. This is why I loved being a sportscaster, and I wanted to use this passion to rebuild my business.

From the beginning, it seemed like a natural fit, and I was determined that this franchise would kill two birds with one stone. It would highlight what I love most about reporting and allow me to pivot within my business.

My first target was the legendary Bobby Bowden. Bowden was among the best college football coaches ever. He was also among the most accessible, if not the most accessible. Even at the height of his successful run as coach at Florida State University, you could find his home phone number amazingly in the phone book under Robert Bowden. And the door to his home was always open, even to reporters. In a pinch, he would routinely let me and a crew come to his house for a quick interview. Bowden was always accommodating, whether after a practice or during the most stressful situations following a tough loss.

So, when the idea of "Errands" came to my mind, I immediately thought Bowden should kick off this series. The first move was to call Bowden's home. On my first try, his wife, Ann, answered. I explained my idea, and she told me that he was out of town at a speaking engagement, but to call him the following week, which I did. When I pitched the idea to Bobby, he liked it and suggested a few errands he would like to run. He said we could pick up his dry cleaning and go for his daily morning walk on the golf course he lived on. I thought that was perfect, so we scheduled the shoot for two months down the road, which gave me time to get a local Tallahassee car dealership to sponsor it. As we concluded our initial discussion, I told Bowden I would check in with him in a month, which I did. He was still enthusiastic.

Fast forward to the week of the shoot, with a sponsor and a crew ready to go, I called Bowden to finalize the specifics, but Bowden had a surprise. He was having second thoughts. Often, the problem with ideas like these, especially when you start, is you don't have anything tangible to show those you want to participate. I had never shot an "Errands" episode, but I knew if we got Bowden, it would jolt the project into a new stratosphere. An episode with such a big name and likable personality would motivate other networks and teams to participate. That was the goal.

Not having a prior episode to show Bowden made him wonder what he was getting into. Combine that with the fact he was approaching his 90s, and I got the sense he and his family were concerned about how Bobby would be portrayed. Though I tried to get him to reconsider, Bowden didn't want to do it, and after all he had done for me over the years, I couldn't hold any ill will towards him for that. It was disappointing because I knew he would have been the perfect candidate to kick off the series. To this day, I still have the voided check from the Tallahassee car dealership on my desk. It motivates me whenever I hit a speed bump with this project or any project.

Don't give up on your dreams. I didn't give up on "Errands."

At that point, I wondered if my "Errands" idea would make it. I had faith in the concept, though, and I wasn't about to quit there without giving it the shot I felt it deserved. So, I thought of another candidate who would be just as good, if not better than Bowden. I thought of legendary college basketball analyst Dick Vitale, who is as animated and affable as they come.

If you think this former coach and Hall of Fame Sportscaster's on-air schtick isn't genuine, think again. Nothing could be further from the truth. In my brief experiences with him over the years, Vitale was always the real deal. After college, when I was an intern with the Cardinals, I got Dick tickets to a spring training game. I remember him taking my address then, but I never thought much about it. A few weeks later, I received a thoughtful handwritten letter and a signed book. A few years later, as a local sports anchor in Tallahassee, I had Vitale join me for a live shot before an FSU basketball game. He could not have been more accommodating. This man seemingly makes time for everyone, making him a perfect candidate for my "Errands" series.

I first mentioned that to him during an event we both attended. He gave me the contact information for his public relations team, and after a few correspondences, he agreed to be the inaugural "Errands" guest. Then things got even more exciting because, just as I had with Bowden, I had to find a sponsor to make this work.

Once again, I thought a car dealership was the perfect sponsor to sell this series. As soon as Vitale was on board, I immediately pursued nearly every car dealer in his hometown of Sarasota. I called them all: Honda, Kia, Nissan, etc. Oddly, the only dealership to call me back was Mercedes, and on the day of the shoot, the General Manager of Mercedes-Benz Sarasota, Ernie Withers, followed up by sweetening the deal. He was going to have me drive Vitale around in a G-Wagon. I'm not a big car guy, but it was a sign the sponsor was into it as much as I was.

As expected, Vitale was everything I could have asked for and more. He was energetic yet revealing at the same time. For a man who has done thousands of interviews, his sincerity for this project was appreciated. Our errands included reading the morning paper at his home, watching his grandchildren play tennis, and attending a meeting with his fundraising team, which has raised millions of dollars for pediatric cancer. Vitale will forever be the godfather of "Errands," a man who, to borrow his words, is "Awesome with a capital A."

Funny, but as fulfilling as it was to land Vitale, I hit my share of roadblocks in the following months with this project. That is until an exciting moment happened while I was hosting a pregame show in Atlanta before a Saints-Falcons NFL game. The Saints Vice President of Digital Media, Doug Tatum, approached me and told me he saw the Vitale episode of "Errands" and wondered if I could host and produce those for the Saints' platforms. Like the Drew Brees sharpie story, I was blown away at the potential opportunity.

What developed from that brief conversation was a partnership between my company and the New Orleans Saints that forever changed the direction of the "Errands" series, my faith as an entrepreneur, and the art of pivoting. The Saints offered me a deal similar to one they would offer an NFL player. It was a two-year deal with a one-year option, a prove-it deal. If we could produce a product that met their expectations in Year One, we would get renewed for Year Two.

Well, Year One proved to be a big success. We succeeded in giving the Saints content they were happy with. Along the way, I was thinking about how satisfying this was. I created "Errands" out of desperation. With my company forced to pivot from years of serving nonprofits, my idea replaced that work and gave me the confidence I could produce more creative projects in the future.

The lesson: When you think you've hit a dead end, always remember you are never out of options. Trust your instincts and move forward! The key is to pursue something you enjoy and lean on what you do well.

The great thing about working with the Saints was I didn't have to sell the series as I had with Dick Vitale. The team had aligned "Errands" with Bridgestone Tires, who liked our work so much that they used it nationally as a template when discussing creative digital marketing projects. After our two-year deal was up, we were re-signed for two more years. We even made it work during the COVID-19 pandemic.

I wondered how we would keep this going at the height of that pandemic. I followed my advice—it was time for more cold calls. I placed one to legendary Saints quarterback Archie Manning, the father of NFL quarterbacks Peyton and Eli Manning. Archie and I had worked in several Saints preseason telecasts before, but it had been well over a decade since we'd done anything together. When I called him, he was on an elliptical machine working out, but he stopped and told me he wanted to hear what my series was about. After my brief pitch, Archie said he liked the idea and agreed to it. Less than a month later, I drove Archie Manning around New Orleans with our masks on, running errands. We made it work during the pandemic. It all was a result of a cold call. Again—it only takes one!

Someone I respect in the media asked me how I got Archie Manning to do that. My answer: I asked. It's as simple as that.

Manning's "Errands" episode was one of 25 we hosted and produced for the Saints, who extended our deal three times over a five-year span. The "Errands" experience brought together nearly all the lessons I try to pass on in this book:

- **Do something that scares you:** I was scared to launch something so different, but I believed in my work and had faith it would be a segment sports fans would enjoy. It was a good idea on paper and in my mind, and we proved it was good on air when we executed it with Vitale. That is a scary process, but getting results builds confidence and increases your tendency to trust your instincts in future projects.
- **It's OK to Quit, but you better have a plan:** We had to quit devoting so much of our time to bringing in nonprofit work, as it was trending downward, but we had a plan, and "Errands" delivered beyond my expectations. As I've repeatedly emphasized in this book, don't ever lose faith in what made you successful. Often, though, you must pivot from your passion to find success, which was the case in this project.
- **It only takes one to love you! Don't be afraid to ask**: Dick Vitale proved to be the perfect candidate to launch the series, but I had to make the initial ask. His cooperation reinforced that it only takes one to make it happen. I believed in this mantra before launching "Errands," but the success of this project reinforced my faith in putting yourself out there.
- **Maximize Relationships:** Before I started my "Errands" series, I had covered the New Orleans Saints for 13 seasons. During that time, the organization had seen my work for years, so I had earned credibility and respect and built a rapport with several of the former Saints players I had covered. This enabled me to earn their trust, host, and launch this project. Much like my dealing with Drew Brees, which started with a

sharpie and led to 14 years of exclusive access and a successful book, "Errands" was a byproduct of getting the most out of relationships I had forged for over a decade.
- **Cold Calls are still a thing:** I can't tell you how many cold calls I made to book guests in my "Errands" series. Like my business, not all of them were successful, but like my previous efforts, most were receptive and ultimately led to quality results.

PASSION CHASERS

Comedians are a different breed.

Like most performers, many must lean on their passion to survive the massive rejection during their humble beginnings. Loving their craft gets them through the tough years. I referenced Dave Grohl's ride to superstardom, which included many nights in sleeping bags, the back of cars, and cheap hotel rooms. For comedians, the origins of their passion are often small crowds in clubs where they have to prove their mettle to a room full of strangers. It's a challenge that would quickly destroy many, but for these funny people, loving what they do and having the chance to do it for a living gets them through it.

One of the most respected comedians of all time, George Carlin, survived one of those against-all-odds journeys. It was detailed in the HBO documentary on his life, "George Carlin's American Dream." The documentary highlighted the many ups and downs of his personal and professional life, including drug addiction and his wife's alcoholism. Initially, Carlin was a mainstream talent who gained notoriety as a gifted, funny man while appearing on prime-time television shows in the 60s. Uncomfortable in those formats, he became a renegade in the 70s, where he let his hair down both literally and figuratively. This drastic pivot allowed him to broaden his routine to touch on more radical topics, including politics. By the 80s, though, Carlin had become typecast as a comic. His routine had become stale. So, he pivoted again to prove his critics wrong and reinvented himself with several legendary and high successful HBO comedy specials.

What got him through a career where he almost lost everything yet rebounded repeatedly? His passion for what he loved.

"If you follow your heart, if you do the right thing, if you do what's on your mind and in your heart and your brain, good things will happen, good things will come." Carlin said in his HBO documentary.

Carlin's numerous career pivots made him one of the most admired comics among his peers, but money was never the driver. He loved what he did and all that came with it. His agent, Jeff Walk, was with him for much of his long and winding comedic road and attested to that in "George Carlin's American Dream."

"He liked money, he liked spending it, but the money was not everything to him," Walk said, "The work was. His writing, his ability to put his ideas out there."

THE MONEY WILL COME

Comedian Jerry Seinfeld's net worth surpasses one billion, but his passion for comedy supersedes money. Seinfeld never thought he'd have this kind of wealth, most of which was earned through the production of his self-titled TV show. "Seinfeld" stopped taping in 1998, yet this comedian has never stopped working.

Why? Because his passion for standup comedy never waned.

"I'm very dedicated to my little craft of standup. I still find it challenging," Seinfeld said on the "Smartless" podcast in 2021.

Seinfeld can do anything he wants, yet he still enjoys his passion for making people laugh. It remains a challenge that he takes on daily in an office where he makes it a point to write every morning. He still cares about the quality of his work, which he tries out in various New York City comedy clubs. The fact that he still grinds it out in his 60s surprises his peers, who are old enough to be his children.

"I think they think it's weird. They don't understand why I'm there, why I would be doing this?" Seinfeld told "Smartless." "You already have money. Why are you bothering with this? That's what they think."

Seinfeld's passion for comedy came early. He told "Smartless" that he remembered writing and delivering his first joke.

"I wrote this joke and I told it to some guys in college," he said. "It was my bit about being left-handed is always associated with negative things: two left-handed feet, a left-handed compliment. You go to a party. There is nobody there. Where did everyone go? They left.

"That is the first joke I ever wrote and these guys they laughed, and I was shocked because I really never thought I could be a comedian. It was like wishing to be an astronaut or a baseball player. You can't do that, really people can't do that.

"I didn't even know what they were doing. I didn't understand. How do they talk in a series of jokes? I thought maybe they were just like that all the time. I thought they were geniuses."

Growing up in Brooklyn, New York, money was never the motivator to make a living making people laugh. His passion originated from his father. In comedian David Steinberg's book, "Inside Comedy," Steinberg passed on the moment when the light bulb went off for him. "When Jerry Seinfeld was eight years old, he remembers a day when he was watching television with his family, and a comedian was on, and he was telling stories, and his dad said, "See that guy on the TV? His actual job is to be funny."

The rest was history.

Before he was a star, Jerome Seinfeld graduated from college with a degree in communications and theater and found his path after falling in love with the art of standup comedy. After graduating from college, he became Jerry Seinfeld, who soon mastered many open-mic nights and saw his first break come from appearing in TV sitcoms years before he would have his own.

A turning point in Seinfeld's pivot towards his passion was a three-episode stint on the TV show, "Benson."

"And then I got fired," Seinfeld told Steinberg. "The part was so small, and I was so irrelevant to the show that they didn't even bother to tell me."

It was an embarrassing moment for Seinfeld, but instead of letting it deter him from following his dream, it motivated this future star to pursue his passion even harder.

"That was one of the great experiences that I had," he told Steinberg, "because it made me so angry that they had the power to just take this away from me. And I started focusing on writing and working hard and saying I'm going to be a comedian because they can't take that away."

From that moment on, Seinfeld became known as a comedian who loved everything about the profession. He loved perfecting his material and practicing his routines in comedy clubs, big and small. His goal wasn't to make millions, and it wasn't to become famous. Seinfeld simply wanted to be great at being a comedian. That was it.

David Steinberg hits on the crux of Seinfeld's passion as someone who followed his career and worked with him on several projects, including his legendary TV show. Steinberg's response tells you everything when asked why Seinfeld returned to doing stand-up and traveling around the country even after all the fortune and fame.

"It is really so simple," Steinberg writes in "Inside Comedy." "He loves it. Purely, totally, in a way perhaps only other comedians can understand. The joy he gets from the challenge of making people laugh sends him back on the road to practice his craft. Whether it is in a club for twenty people or in an arena for thousands—simply, it is where he is happiest."

Earlier in this book, I outlined the career passion path of musician Dave Grohl. At the crossroads as a high school dropout and given his first big break to work with an established band, he asked his Mom for advice. She told him, "You better be good." Like Grohl, Seinfeld was dedicated and confident he could succeed. Those are two qualities you must have to endure all your potential passion throws at you.

"People watch me do stand-up, after all my success, watch the documentary about my tours, and think it is so hard. Really?" Seinfeld says in "Inside Comedy." "It isn't hard at all unless you're not good at it, and if you are not good at it, then it is the hardest job in the world. But if you can do it, it's really kind of fun and easy."

A valuable lesson: Find what you are good at, believe in yourself, and go for it!

Seinfeld's passion for comedy proves that if you love something, as my Dad often told me growing up, "Then the money will come." I firmly believe Seinfeld never thought he would become the billionaire he is, and I admire that his love for standup comedy is so strong that he would be doing it regardless of what kind of money he made.

Seinfeld never wanted to leave his first love, but he saw an opportunity to broaden his brand and pivoted to network television. "Seinfeld" was not a success out of the gates, though. It was rejected by FOX and NBC, which only made room for it after canceling a Bob Hope special. At first, the critics loved "Seinfeld," but viewers ignored it. The ratings were awful early on, yet patience paid off as the show produced 180 episodes in a remarkable nine-year run.

One of the most popular television shows in history, "Seinfeld," finished its run by ranking in the top two in ratings alongside the famous "ER" series from 1994 to 1998. Only two other shows in American television history, "I Love Lucy" and "The Andy Griffith Show," finished their stellar runs at the top of the rating heap.

Seinfeld's name will forever be tied to one of television's greatest shows, a far cry from his original expectations.

"I never thought I would do anything like that, and when we were doing the show, I thought, 'This has a chance to be a little niche thing that might survive on an obscure time slot somewhere,'" Seinfeld reflected on the "Smartless" podcast. "When the show became a big hit, it became a big shock to me."

Pivoting allowed Seinfeld to build his brand and perfect his craft. When he left the sitcom, he knew he had gotten everything he could from the experience.

PIVOTING FROM "RIDICULOUSNESS"

For Seinfeld, his profitable pivot to television was satisfying. Still, it couldn't equal his insatiable love for stand-up, which always superseded any notoriety he garnered as the lead man for one of the most acclaimed TV shows ever. He easily could have ridden off into the sunset after all the millions he made from his TV show, but that never crossed his mind. To his credit, Seinfeld's consuming drive to perfect his passion had him performing in small comedy clubs full of 20 fans and then graduating to sold-out arenas full of thousands. It wasn't about the money. It was about the drive to pursue what he loved, as Seinfeld shared with Steinberg his mindset after becoming one of the most acclaimed TV stars we've ever seen.

"It was so unlikely! I mean, what happened to me was ridiculous," he said. "That was not the plan. The plan was to do the TV show, hang on for a couple, two, three years. Like an obscure little cult thing. And I'll pump up my ticket sales at the comedy clubs. That's why I called it *Seinfeld*. I thought, 'Well, at least I'll sell some tickets.'

"Stand-up is the most intimate performance, I think, that there is. That relationship, when it's locked in, is so intense, and rich, that all of the negative things about comedy that people say—how difficult it is, how humiliating it can be—I embrace all that. Because I think the ledger still tips in our favor. You get so much. And you're also so much more in control of your life and your destiny and your art," he said in "Inside Comedy."

The art of stand-up still drives Seinfeld, who isn't working for the weekend. After all his success, he is still working to perfect his passion.

"Yeah it's a lot of work, but I'm lucky that I love the work and I'm willing to do it," he told "Smartless." "I like the simplicity and the independence of it. It's very hard to sustain if you don't keep at it."

Passion is crucial, but the key component in any career pivot is using skills you have acquired over many years. Seinfeld agrees as he told New Yorker magazine writer David Remnick, "The only thing in life that's really worth having is good skill. Good skill is the greatest possession. The things that money buys are fine. They're good. I like them. But having a skill, it's a very Zen Buddhist concept: Pursue Mastery. That will fulfill your life. You will feel good. I know a lot of rich people. They don't feel good, as you think they should and would. They're miserable because if they don't master a skill, life is unfulfilling."

The lesson: Maximizing your life comes down to maximizing your potential. We all have acquired skills to reach our potential; it's upon us to harness those skills into a career full of happiness.

No comedian may have pivoted from their passion more than Steve Martin. Always a performer, Martin went from being one of the most popular comedians to starring in several movies, but at the end of his career, he created even more options. In his 70s, Martin kept with his comedic roots by traveling around the United States with old friend and fellow comic Martin Short. Still, Martin also pivoted towards other passions, which included writing and music.

As a famous comic, Martin's signature all-white suit was legendary, but so was his trusty banjo, which was always by his side. Like many actors who later go behind the camera to become successful producers and directors, Martin shifted to his music roots after years of starring in movies. He wrote Broadway musicals and then grabbed his banjo to release an aptly named, "The Long-Awaited Album."

Martin was first introduced to the banjo when he was 15, growing up in California, where his performing roots took shape working at Disneyland. Growing up in the 50s, he developed his fondness for playing by working with high school classmate John McEuen, who would go on to great success as a part of the Nitty Gritty Dirt Band. At the time, Martin's favorite music genre was bluegrass, played by the Foggy Mountain Boys featuring guitarist Lester Flatt and banjo player Earl Scruggs. After years of success in comedy and acting, Martin craved a return to his musical roots, where his fame ironically reunited him with his childhood idol.

Martin told Newsweek's Zach Schonfeld that he got the itch to pivot towards his new musical passion by reuniting with Scruggs in the early 2000s.

"The great banjo player, Earl Scruggs, was doing an album, and he asked me to play on it. And I did," Martin told Newsweek. There's a famous bluegrass song called "Foggy Mountain Breakroom" that Earl Scruggs wrote. We were going to play "Foggy Mountain Breakdown." I was always a very fast banjo player, but I realized I had slowed down a little bit, and I wanted to pick it back up again. It just got me interested in the banjo. I started practicing more and got more speed back."

The pivot from his passion paid off for Martin, who took the time to perfect his old/new love and released his first music album, "The Crow," which won a Grammy in 2010. His second offering was a collaboration with the Steep Canyon Rangers, whom Martin toured with for a while following the release. That led to an invitation to play at the U.S. Capitol in Washington, D.C. on the fourth of July 2011 in front of one of the largest audiences ever for a bluegrass band. Martin's continued work at his newfound craft would get further recognition when he and the Steep Canyon Rangers were named the 2011 entertainers of the year in the most significant award given by the International Bluegrass Music Association Awards in Nashville.

A powerful lesson rings true yet again here. You can love what you do but still pivot from your passion. Martin enjoyed being a standup comedian and a standout leading man for much of his career, yet basked in the glow of later pivoting to his musical roots, making his life more complete.

When asked by Newsweek if he is quitting movies for good? Martin's response was proof of how much he has embraced his latest career shift.

"I don't really think about movies," he said. "I'm so happy doing what I'm doing."

Picking up his old friend, the banjo, added a new element to a career soundtrack that Martin has been strumming for decades.

"It's perfectly convenient, and I don't have to leave the family," he said.

Comedians, like lawyers or doctors, can take unexpected, unpredictable, yet ultra-fulfilling career paths. Martin's powerful pivot to music culminated in a career during which he learned something new with every step he took.

"I think that experience is your greatest asset, meaning you have to take every job no matter how horrible it is," he said.

Martin, Seinfeld, and Carlin would agree that life is less horrible if you love what you do.

PIVOTING FROM PASSION ... TO PASSION

Justin is a respected colleague who grew up with a passion for sports and money, specifically investing money.

As a teenager, Justin will never forget where he learned the value of saving a buck. His grandmother instilled it in him.

"I'll never forget when we were kids growing up," he told me. "She would say, 'Justin, you max out your Ira.' She didn't call it an IRA. She called it an 'Ira.' You're a kid. You don't know what the heck grandma is talking about."

Yet hearing grandma's constant references to the valued "Ira" impacted young Justin, who admits over time, he took to heart his grandmother's lessons about "compounding interests and the importance of investing when you're younger."

As he matured, Justin became more curious about the value of the ole "Ira." He read up on it in high school and quickly became interested. What further sold him on the importance of saving money was watching his grandmother, who worked double shifts her whole life, and his parents who put a premium on protecting what you earn. Growing up with a stay-at-home mother and a father who worked as a mailman, he noticed how they could provide as well for him as his friends' parents, who were doctors and lawyers, provided for their children. The secret was long-term investing, and Justin became fascinated to the point that he started investing himself.

"I opened up my first IRA when I was 17 years old, put a couple of hundred bucks in it, and that was right before the great recession in 2008," Justin explained.

At the time, Justin saw his small investment cut in half, which seemed like the end of the world. Ironically, this short-term investment turned out to be a glimpse into what one day would be his long-term future. The moment's perspective was a valuable teacher.

"I saw a couple of hundred bucks get cut in half and thought it was the worst thing ever, and wondered, 'Oh my god, how do people do this?'" Justin remembered. "Meanwhile, people are losing millions of dollars at the time. It was my crash course on the market and long-term focus where I learned with a couple of hundred bucks instead of hundreds of thousands, if not millions. I think that helped prepare me for the future and gave me an understanding that investing doesn't happen over one or two years. It happens over decades."

Justin quickly became fascinated with the investment world, but at the time, he had a bigger priority. He wanted to fulfill his dream of becoming a big-time sportscaster.

"We all wanted to get to ESPN," he said. "We all wanted to live out this dream."

Justin's dream became a reality as he climbed the latter from a small market in Winchester, Virginia, to a medium market in Rochester, New York, and then to a top-tier market in Tampa, Florida.

"I had an amazing time at all three stops," Justin said, reflecting on his broadcast journey. "I covered a World Series. I covered a National Championship, The NCAA Final Four. It was an incredible experience in gaining the confidence I have now."

But fulfilling his dream was bittersweet for Justin, who found that being a sportscaster wasn't everything he had initially envisioned.

"This might sound like sour grapes, but I don't BS," he said. "I give it to everyone straight. TV is not merit-based. They're looking for something that isn't necessarily talent all the time, which really turned me off."

Justin found sportscasting wasn't the end game he expected, but he was primed for his ultimate pivot, which proved to be a seamless career maneuver. He may have put his passion for investing on the back burner, but his drive to be a financial advisor was always something he thought would be a viable option.

"Becoming a financial advisor was in the pipeline for me for many years," Justin said upon reflection. "I just didn't pull the trigger until I saw certain mentors that were older, at jobs most of us could only dream of, being told they were being let go. Not because of talent or work ethic but for other factors."

Few would leave a job as a successful sportscaster in a burgeoning sports market, but Justin believed his pivot into the financial world wasn't a fly-by-night affair. It was something he had thought about for years. A central tenet in this book is, it's OK to quit, but you better have a plan.

Justin executed that perfectly.

"If your intentions are good, you will succeed," Justin said. "If you can pivot and do it for the right reasons, whether it's to support your family or a passion, you will find success. It could take time, but you will be fine if you have good intentions."

Justin pivoted at a pivotal moment—just as he and his wife were welcoming their first child. While this transition may seem risky for some, his story proves that if you pivot into a new passion, it creates more security and often elicits more happiness.

"I would say I came up short of the goals and aspirations I had (in sportscasting)," Justin said. "But I am more than happy to admit that because that led me to ultimately the dream I didn't realize I had at the time, which was to be that financial advisor.

"The way the (sportscasting) business changed really turned me off because it's no longer merit-based. The beauty of my job is it's completely merit based. I do right by my clients, I listen to them, and I service them properly. The sky is the absolute limit."

Justin knew he could continue as a sportscaster. He still had options. But the upside wasn't as great as he envisioned it would be with his new passion. He didn't just want to hold on to his first dream. So he pivoted, knowing his new endeavor had the potential to be more fulfilling. Making the move wasn't easy, but ironically, his time as a sportscaster spurred his leap of faith.

We see a common theme in pivoting towards your passion: those who lean on the skills they have acquired to benefit them in their new endeavors!

Justin's skills as a sportscaster were instrumental to his success as a financial advisor.

"It provided me with the communication skills I have now," he said. "Without those ten years in sports, there's no way I would be a successful financial advisor. I say that with the utmost confidence because of all the things broadcasting provided me. Maybe I didn't get to where I wanted to be (in sportscasting) but without it, I wouldn't be where I am today."

Through sportscasting, Justin learned how to work long hours and how to communicate effectively with people, two qualities that he used in making his successful transfer to the financial world.

"As a financial advisor, I like to call myself the CFO of my clients," Justin said. "So whether that's getting a mortgage, purchasing a car, or physically investing their money, I tell my clients, 'Let me be responsible for that for you. Let me guide you. Let me give you your best options.' I'm not gonna tell you, 'You must do this,' but I am going to give you multiple options and tell you what I believe is best. Anything across the board with a dollar sign in front of it, I feel like it's my responsibility to help my clients."

As a local sportscaster, your days are rarely the same, and your hours are long and unpredictable. Having performed well under those conditions was an excellent prerequisite for Justin's new role.

"I think that has really set me apart from other young financial advisors," he said. "We can all say that we grind and work hard. TV people work hard. They grind. They might not have the income of other career paths if they don't reach certain levels, but the work ethic and the grind in the profession is so natural in news and in journalism (in terms of) nights, holidays, and weekends. You move around and don't see family. These are sacrifices we all make. You don't make those sacrifices in other jobs, so I think that separated me."

When he took over as an advisor, Justin quickly realized how his ability to adjust to the day-to-day schedule in the media world would serve him well in the financial world.

"I think the work ethic in newsrooms and being more than willing to make those sacrifices, I can honestly say, myself and my financial team, we put in significantly more hours than most financial advisors because to me it's natural," he said.

Communicating effectively and enduring long hours is great, but Justin discovered other traits that assisted him in his pivot. Little things in his old career became prominent in his new one, specifically for his growing list of clients.

"I don't mind taking a phone call for a client on a weekend," he said. "Most financial advisors don't do that. I do because I worked weekends almost my entire life (in television)."

It was a seamless pivot for Justin, who quickly found his previous skills were invaluable. At the core of it was the confidence he developed as a sportscaster.

"If I can command a camera in a region as large as the Tampa Bay market, I can sit one-on-one with someone who has $10 million and confidently express to them the long-term plan we have in place that will work for the long-term," he said. "It's because I could step in front of a camera and never feel nervous or second guess myself."

Anchoring a sportscast and reading the news was one thing, but Justin's pivot enabled him to take on a more significant role.

"The difference now is I'm part of events," he said. "I'm on those boards, such as the American Cancer Society, or I'm at the Chamber of Commerce. It's a different level of being in the community."

For some, the pivot could be the reverse. They could go from the private sector to the media or in several different directions. The clear message in Justin's case is that if you find what you like, the choice is yours. Just discover something you enjoy and do well. Justin's inspiration was his wife, a reporter who pivoted to become a successful communications officer.

"If she had the courage to do it," he said, "then I could find the courage to do it."

The lesson: Never stop loving what you do. Just find other ways to do it!

For years, Justin felt satisfaction from breaking or telling a unique sports story. Now, his relationships have a deeper meaning.

"I have clients who say, 'Hey, if I can make X amount of money, do you think that's a good idea?'" he said. "If I do right by them because I know long term it's going to help them significantly, I hit a home run that day. Even though I didn't make money that day, I did right by some, and that is going to come full circle because there are a lot of financial advisors out there who would have taken the money instead of telling them to put it in a better place. That's just the passion I have to help people with their finances."

Doing right by people fulfills Justin, another example of how having one dream in life doesn't prohibit you from pivoting to another.

"In TV, we can affect a lot of change and help a lot of people," Justin said. "We can tell stories. I'm now doing it differently, and for me at least, it's so much more tangible the impact I'm making on people now, and I love that.

"To me, taking that leap of faith and doing it for the right reasons, I'm really grateful I did that."

The pivot has paid off for this former sportscaster turned financial advisor, as Justin has found immediate success. He's routinely among the top ten in his region in bringing in net new assets.

Another "pivotal" success story!

CHAPTER EIGHT

BUILD ON YOUR FOUNDATION

"The only way to do great work is to love what you do."
Steve Jobs

When you build something, you start with the foundation. Your foundation is at the core of everything this book represents. We all have foundations. It doesn't matter which profession you're in or how old you are. We have built a skill set and developed a passion that enables us all to pivot. Pivoting should be a word that lends itself to new beginnings, a continuation of something we love, yet channeling it in a newfound direction. Change is difficult, but if you use your foundation to make that change, the possibilities are endless and often exciting.

It's normal to question the relevance of your foundation because it's something we take for granted. We all possess skills we have honed for years yet don't fully appreciate. These attributes are often built-up strengths that you thought pertained to one specific job, but this book aims to take a closer look at your foundation and discover new ways to use your skills that you never imagined.

Exciting, right?

I challenge all of you to put this book down for a second, grab a pen and paper, and write down five qualities you have accrued over your lifetime that are part of your foundation! Think hard—they could be anything, but you are looking for something specific that

would benefit you if you pivot towards a new passion.
Your five best work-related qualities

(1)

(2)

(3)

(4)

(5)

Recently, I asked a friend in his 50s who had been laid off, "If you could do or be anything, what would it be?"

He is a longtime accountant and quickly responded, "I'd be a boat captain."

I told him, "So why don't you put some thought into it?"

He laughed at the notion, a common response for many when thinking about doing something they would truly love, but I was serious. Your dreams and ultimate passions may be far-fetched in your mind, but your foundation enables you to pursue anything.

Don't limit your dreams!

Pro Football Hall of Famer Michael Strahan personifies pivoting. He has been so successful since leaving the game that many forgot he played because they now know him as a multi-media television personality. While many athletes search for something that will satisfy them as much as their athletic careers, Strahan always knew he was more than just a football player.

Pivoting was always going to be a part of his game plan.

"I never looked at football as the only thing I can do, and I think because of that mindset, it's allowed me to not handicap myself, not allowed me to put myself in such a box that this is it, and that's all," Strahan told Rich Eisen in his "Voices of the NFL" podcast.

The box Strahan references is a boundary of limitations many of us put on ourselves regarding what we can accomplish. For Strahan, the box has no limits.

"I'm more like, 'Ok, football was a start,'" he said. "The box is wide open; no end, no size on the box, just go. Fill the box instead of having the box tell you what you can put it in. You put as much as you can into the box."

Exploring your possibilities can be an awakening that leads to the kind of happiness you couldn't possibly realize. Many, including Strahan, have unraveled a second chance, leading to a new feeling of freedom. Strahan's many pivots to new passions have him working harder than ever, but he's loving every minute.

"I do it because I love it," he told Eisen. "It's so much fun. I don't have a bad job, and I really mean that."

Waking up at the crack of dawn to join the "Good Morning America" (GMA) team and then flying across the country to join his partners at Fox Sports every weekend during football season makes for a long week. Sure, it's a lot of work, but for Strahan, it isn't.

"I do not have a job that I go to in the morning (even GMA early) and think, 'I don't want to be here.' I get there, and I'm energized. I'm excited."

Some are in careers where they never see a need to pivot. They love what they do and don't need to change, or they work for the same employer from college until retirement. But that scenario is becoming less and less commonplace.

Many still love what they do, but different obstacles get in the way. It could be a layoff, a family matter, or a change in the direction of the vocation. These roadblocks can put your pivot on "pause," but that doesn't mean you can't push "play" when the time is right for you to shift to a better option.

Life is unpredictable. And you don't have to stay in one lane. Happiness can be found elsewhere if you're willing to take the plunge.

Some people go through life counting down the days to retirement yet fail to realize all the potential inside them, the potential that could lead to the happiness they've always wanted. Often, they feel it's too late to grab the wheel and steer in a new direction. They fail to see the opportunities that pivoting toward a new career presents. Many believe their dreams aren't practical or couldn't possibly reward them financially. These beliefs are misnomers and easy excuses for some to stay in a situation where they grow stale and remain unchallenged. It's easy not to pivot, not to take the chance, but you may be missing out on the potential rewards.

I've used different examples of passion in this book. The common thread is that everyone I referenced as an example would do what they do without the millions they have made. Their love of their crafts supersedes the money they make. Tony Hawk would still be skateboarding if he wasn't a multi-millionaire. I trust Dave Grohl would be drumming, singing, or playing somewhere in this world, even if he hadn't found considerable fame and fortune. I appreciate that Randall Gay would be practicing law and helping his community even if he hadn't found success as an NFL player. I'm confident Jerry Seinfeld would still be doing stand-up if he hadn't been the namesake of one of the most popular TV shows in history.

It doesn't mean we don't want money or crave material possessions. But often, if we find our passion, the money comes with it. Hawk, Grohl, Gay, and Seinfeld are proof. So am I. My first job in television paid $12,000. I didn't bat an eye when I learned that because I knew the opportunity was far greater than the paycheck. Then, shortly after taking the job, I was given a promotion that "elevated" my salary to $15,000 a year. Soon thereafter, I was offered a part-time radio job, which elevated my salary to $30,000. I doubled my money in a year and felt like a millionaire because I was doing what I loved. You can't put a price on doing something you truly love every day.

Has my work life been full of smiles every day? Absolutely not! At one point, I endured three layoffs in four years. There were plenty of opportunities to quit and move along.

But I refused to give into a career that wasn't satisfying.

I pivoted and started a business that has had its share of ups and downs, but because I love it and refused to quit, I discovered many ways to survive and thrive. At the age of 50, I went back to school, and despite sometimes wondering what I was doing there at that stage in my life, the decision paid off, leading to a fulfilling teaching career. At the same time, I published my first book and started a public speaking career. With every move, the one constant was a calculated step toward something I would ultimately enjoy. Whether reporting, creating, teaching, speaking, or writing, I have loved every option much more than if I had settled for the status quo. I never wanted to look back with regret, and I don't want you to either.

This book intentionally complements all of my pivoting pointers with examples of real people who have found success by following their passion and pivoting toward it. The intended message: if they can do it, you can too! I created two major themes. A string of success stories highlights the "passion chasers" who have achieved ultimate success by never deviating from what they love. The second theme is those who have "pivoted to success." They started with a dream but, after facing different obstacles and realizations in their lives, were able to shift to new and more fulfilling careers.

Every vocation has those who have pivoted to greener pastures, but for our purposes, I chose to feature a group of sportscasters, all of whom grew up with one main goal: covering sports. Like me, several of my peers never thought they would pivot away from their initial dreams to sell Goop Dogs and real estate, launch an auctioneering company, or become a financial advisor. Although I picked a group of sportscasters, I guarantee I could find a group of accountants, doctors, or lawyers who have pivoted to success, too.

I want to bring all the book's themes together, and I'll do that by offering two similar examples of pivoting from two different points of view. These two examples prove that happiness can be found in several ways, but you must put yourself out there to make it happen. Although they took different paths in reaching their newfound success, both followed the roadmap in this book, and both agreed that the journey far exceeded their expectations.

PIVOTING TO SUCCESS

As a kid, Pete Cataldo was consumed with sports and soon developed a drive to cover sports for a living. His father, Steve, nurtured his passion and planted the seed while his son was still young.

"I remember fondly sitting down and my Dad introducing me to Magic Johnson, and it just clicked," Pete said. "Showtime and the Lakers, I was all in on sports."

Fueled by his passion, Pete attended and graduated from Florida State University, where he was the sports editor of the school paper. Following graduation, he began climbing the sportscasting ladder, making stops in Macon, Georgia, then Jacksonville, Florida.

Along the way, Pete's bond with his father motivated him to succeed. Both were fans of the NBA's Orlando Magic, and when his father was at work, Pete would turn on the game and deliver a play-by-play to keep him updated. Once Cataldo was hired as a local sportscaster, his Dad was the constant comforting support system he could always lean on even when he wasn't there.

"When I eventually got in the business, one of the things that helped me get comfortable on camera was picturing that I was looking at my father and just talking sports with him," Pete confides.

But when his father died from cancer at 65, Pete's passion for being a sportscaster changed. Couple his loss with the climate of local sports dwindling in scope due to cutbacks, Pete knew it was time to pivot.

"It grew tiresome," Pete admitted.

It was time to chase another passion.

PASSION CHASER

The careers of Peter and comedian Gary Shandling amazingly include all the principles for pivoting toward success that I have presented in this book. The HBO documentary based on Shandling's life, "The Zen Diaries of Gary Shandling," profiles someone who found success by repeatedly taking on career shifts to keep his passion for comedy alive.

Shandling grew up in Tucson, Arizona, where his exposure to standup comedy was limited.

"I never met anyone while I was growing up that was interested in any phase of comedy," Shandling told Entertainment Weekly. "Had there been any clubs, there was a chance I would have started earlier in standup comedy. But there was no outlet for me as a comedian. I thought I was crazy to even consider becoming a comic."

The future comedian enrolled at Arizona State, where he majored in engineering. Then, after three years of study in the intense discipline, Shandling made his first pivot.

"I (majored in) engineering ... because I was interested in electronics," Shandling told Entertainment Weekly. "But after three years of it, one day, just like in a movie, I walked out of one of my engineering labs to get a drink of water and never walked back in.

"I had to get away."

Shandling's life changed forever after that. After pivoting to a business and creative writing major, he finally put his passion for comedy to practical use. While "sitting in the back row and writing comedy monologues," he discovered what he truly loved, which motivated him to pursue his dreams.

MAKE YOUR TRIP!

I have mentioned in this book the importance of making your trip. It sparked my career at its onset and continued to help elevate it throughout. Setting yourself apart by targeting specific employers is beneficial when you begin your journey. In addition, making the trip to place yourself ahead of the competition helps a great deal. Making the trip, though, can have different meanings for different people. The common denominator is going the extra mile, often leading to more opportunities and creating new paths that bring your true passion into better focus.

Upon his father's passing, Pete knew he needed a change, so he bet on himself and hit the road. His trip symbolized a new and adventurous start during which Pete and his fiancée sold all of their belongings while planning their wedding and drove from Jacksonville to New York City. Once they arrived, the courageous couple spent two months sleeping on a friend's couch until they found footing.

For Pete, there were many risks involved. It was a "Carpe Diem" moment. He was still young and liked the "if you can make it here, you can make it anywhere" challenge New York City represented.

"Let me do this now," he thought. "That was the motivation behind it."

There's a lot to unpack here. Pete left a stable career that he had worked hard to build but suddenly gave up everything for the chance to pivot toward greater happiness. It was admirable, but risky, yet it shows how making "your" trip can be a fortuitous step toward finding greater success.

Like Cataldo, Garry Shandling's big break came as a result of hitting the road. While still in college, Shandling saw an opportunity upon learning that George Carlin was appearing at a Phoenix comedy club. So, he made the two-and-a-half-hour drive, hoping to share some of the comedy material he had been working on.

This plan had disaster written all over it. Shandling could have easily been denied the opportunity to meet Carlin, much less show him his work. That's why many would have never embarked on such a journey.

Shandling saw things differently. He knew that making this trip could prove invaluable.

"So I took some routines to Carlin," Shandling told Entertainment Weekly. "He read (them) and said they were really good. He encouraged me to move to Los Angeles."

Not many college students would have made the trip, but Shandling did; the dividends were huge. He connected with Carlin, who inspired him to move to Los Angeles, which Shandling did after graduation in 1972. Success didn't happen instantly (it rarely does), but Los Angeles was the perfect landing spot for Shandling, who got the opportunity to hone his craft and present his work to the right people. Eventually, he landed a job writing comedy for television shows such as "Sanford and Son" and "Welcome Back Kotter."

IT'S OK TO QUIT, BUT YOU BETTER HAVE A PLAN!

A central theme from this book that I want to pass on in terms of building on your foundation is the notion that quitting isn't always bad. As long as you have a plan. The plan could take your career to heights you never realized, something Pete Cataldo would discover via trial and error.

After biding his time on a friend's couch for a few months, Pete did what he thought he should do. Many broadcast journalists who pivot from local news find opportunities in public relations. After pounding the pavement in the Big Apple, which included going door to door and making countless cold calls, Pete found a series of stable yet unfulfilling PR jobs. He described this conventional career move as a "robotic progression." These jobs were sound, but they didn't make him happy. He wasn't passionate about going to them every day.

This is a powerful lesson. We often choose a career or job because we think that's what we need to do in favor of pursuing something that we love.

"Instead of doing the thing that I wanted to do, that I knew I could do, I went and chased the thing I thought I was supposed to do for the money," Pete admitted.

Many of us have dreams in the back of our minds that we would like to pursue but don't act on. After his Dad's death and when he became disenfranchised with being a sportscaster, Pete decided to pursue a career that catered to his true passion, which is fitness.

As a young sportscaster working his first job in Macon, Georgia, Pete had a lot of free time. So, after his local news shows, he started working out late at night at a 24-hour gym. He got in shape, became a certified fitness coach, and started training some of his peers. He did the same during his time in Jacksonville. Pete loved helping people this way but thought, 'Can I really make this a career? No way! It's not realistic!'

Pete is not alone! Many have dreams they would like to pursue but believe they are unrealistic. They're not!

Pete knew sportscasting and public relations jobs would provide stability but not true happiness, so nearly a decade after earning his fitness coach license, he took the plunge, thinking it was now or never.

"At that point, it had been almost 10 years since I first earned that fitness certification, and I was just coaching people on the side," Pete said. "Then I thought, 'I can do this, and not only can I do this, but it will allow me to be creative.'"

Being creative is one of the many skills that helped Pete find success in sportscasting and public relations. We can all use the skills we have acquired in our working lives to ultimately pivot towards our true calling in life.

Finding his creative niche motivated Pete to take the plunge he had waited years to take.

"I missed being creative," he said, "Instead of writing a press release and making up a quote for some random boring CEO, I wanted to create something."

Pete made a nice living as a public relations professional but felt incomplete. He missed the action of doing something different.

"I didn't want to get back into journalism, but I wanted to do something creative," he said.

While Pete thought his initial pivot from sportscasting to public relations would be fulfilling, Gary Shandling's pivot from engineering to comedy seemed seamless. He moved to Los Angeles and became a successful writer, yet he remained restless. After years of writing comedy, Shandling yearned for more. It wasn't enough to write comedy. He wanted to be a comic.

Shandling started to feel the same emotions he experienced at Arizona State's engineering school. He knew there was more out there for him. His dilemma was similar to one we all face. Can you quit something you love in favor of something you could potentially love even more?

"After three years of writing for TV, I couldn't continue," Shandling told Entertainment Weekly. "I couldn't go on. So, I just quit. I was making good money. But it wasn't what I wanted. I called my agent and told him to get me out."

Quitting often has a negative connotation, but it can be bold and liberating if you have a plan. But you have to plan out your next move. Pete and Shandling both had their eyes on a bigger prize, which led to greater happiness in their lives.

DO SOMETHING YOU'RE SCARED OF!

In Pete's shift from sportscasting to PR to fitness coach, a trek where he gave up everything while betting all of it on himself, was there anything that scared him during his bold journey?

"A better question is, was there something that didn't scare me?" Pete said with a laugh. "All of it scared me. I was terrified of leaving the news, but there was a level of confidence that I could still do this."

The lesson: It's okay to be scared and admit it, and, at the end of the day, it's good for you to do something that scares you—it pushes you to greater heights and happiness!

"I packed all my bags and moved to New York City, terrified," Pete said. "I was terrified of starting my own business. It was scary as hell. Now I'm responsible for my paycheck. I gotta go sell myself."

Pete did just that. Boosted by his belief in himself, he has become a thriving personal fitness coach. He has progressed to such a level of comfort that Pete has found his niche and perfect target audience.

"I direct my focus towards busy moms and dads," he said, "I think that, in many ways, the fitness industry is failing moms and dads. It's been my focus to help them become more efficient and show them you don't have to be in the gym all day long. Show them nutrition and that often you're probably overthinking it."

Pete overcame his fears by using the foundation of his previous careers to help him succeed in his ultimate passion. As a fitness coach, he has incorporated many tools he learned in television. Often, as a sportscaster, he was sent out to cover a story, and he had to be both the reporter and the videographer. People like that are called multi-media journalists (MMJs). Now, Pete is an MMJ for his own business.

"It's kind of funny; I started doing one-man bands on camera, editing my video, and I'm essentially doing the same thing now," he said.

But now he doesn't like it. He loves it!

Jumping from writing to performing is scary for anyone, including Garry Shandling. His first professional pivot was a significant jump. From behind the scenes to the eye of the storm, grabbing the spotlight as a standup comedian, he started playing dive bars and clubs like many in that profession. He paid his dues by entering several talent contests and even tried out his act in discos, which were becoming popular then.

The HBO documentary "The Zen Diaries of Garry Shandling" was released two years after his death, so much of the content referenced the many diaries and letters Shandling left behind. Taking the leap of faith from writer to performer was a passion Shandling wanted to pursue, but like so many of us, he was scared to follow his dreams.

His self-doubt was conveyed in letters he wrote to his girlfriend. They revealed a young comic who was scared to take the next step.

"There are a lot of people trying to be funny, and I'm not sure where I stand in the group," Shandling wrote in letters divulged in the documentary. "I consider doing my act every time I'm in the Comedy Store (Los Angeles' elite comedy club) if I could get the guts."

Shandling's lack of confidence serves as a valuable lesson for us all. It's OK to be scared. The key is overcoming your fears and following through, no matter how hard it may seem. This process takes shape in many forms and fashions. It can be done through giving a speech, trying your first case, writing your first book or song—putting yourself out there in many ways. We all go through it! Most people choose to be safe and unhappy in their careers rather than tackle their fears and chase their dreams. Those who do maneuver around their self-doubt are often better for it.

Shandling's fears didn't immediately subside. He admitted to sitting in the back at comedy clubs, watching comedian after comedian and wondering, "My god, who has the nerve to do that."

In his documentary, the then-young comic admitted the rush of adrenaline and relief pouring over him when he finally made his move and overcame his fears.

"God played this great trick on me," he said. "I got some laughs the first time I went on stage, and I walked off that stage, and I thought, 'My God, this could be a way I could find out who I am.'"

Finding success wasn't easy for Shandling, who bombed several times on stage but routinely discovered putting himself out there allowed him to overcome his fears. Even after enduring a near-fatal car crash, Shandling faced a life-defining realization that allowed him to conquer his fears and chase his dreams for good.

"I realized I best try to figure out who I authentically was, and I could do that through standup," he said.

Shandling remembers the defining moment when he knew he had to leave writing and pursue standup comedy full-time.

"I told my writing agent, 'I can't do this,' and he said, 'Do you think you can make it as a comic?' I said, 'I don't know, but if I don't try now, I won't know.'"

Doing something you're scared of is liberating, confidence building and life-defining. It changes everything. I've provided several examples in this book. It's natural to question whether you can do the same. Remember, we all have a foundation. We all have a passion; the foundation enables us to pivot to new desires.

You have to fight the fear.

IT JUST TAKES ONE TO LOVE YOU!

I've stressed the importance of the art of asking. If you don't ask, you won't get results. You don't ask, and you often have to live with the unknown. What if I had asked? What could have happened?

Don't live with regret!

The results can vary, from asking for advice and ways to improve your product to asking a question that allows you to maintain your sanity at the workplace. People generally want to help, so with that in mind, it just takes one person, one mentor, co-worker, or stranger to help you turn it around. My examples of asking Dick Vitale to participate in my "Errands" series and the Tampa Bay Ray mascot DJ Kitty setting in motion my campaign with the Humane Society's PSAs were byproducts of asking. Still, more importantly, they prove that it only takes one to love you. What's important is your aggressive pursuit of that love, which can vary depending on your profession or project.

That one person is personal to each one of us. It could be a boss who believes in you, a stranger with just the right message of hope, a random person who sees your work and, unbeknownst to you, recommends you for the job you've been clamoring for.

Or, in the case of Pete Cataldo, when you put yourself out there in search of your true passion, it could be someone who never left you.

"I think at the end of the day, it was, is, and always will be my father," Pete said. "He believed in me the way no one else has, and he instilled in me that it's always gonna be ok."

Even after his father passed, he lived on in Pete's mind when he left several stable jobs to follow his ultimate dream of becoming a fitness coach. Pete says his bond with his father carried him through the process.

"My Dad would tell me, 'You're not going to be in the street. You're gonna be ok,'" Peter remembered. "He would say, 'You're gonna be ok. Just keep going. I'm always here. I'm always going to love you. I don't care what you do.'"

The most poignant words from father to son were, "So go do it, do the thing, go do the thing."

The lesson: Your one person can come in various ways. Lean on that one person to motivate you and clear a path to happiness—whomever they are. Find them, trust them, and know they are out there, however you come in contact with them. They are a valuable cog in your pivoting to success.

The media world differed when Garry Shandling worked up the comedic ladder. No social media, no YouTube, no internet, and only three major television networks (Fox would come later). For a comedian back then, the one person who could change their life was Johnny Carson. A good five to seven minutes on Carson's "The Tonight Show" could be the ultimate game-changer. It could earn you instant national credibility and translate into top billing at all the marquee comedy clubs in the country.

After a few years of grinding it out on the open-mic scene, Shandling finally got the coveted call to Los Angeles' comedy epicenter, "The

Comedy Store." His agent brought in a "The Tonight Show" talent scout that evening. After seizing the moment, the opportunity and connection opened the door for his big break to showcase his talents to Johnny. The exposure would change his life forever.

The lesson: You must find your Johnny Carson—someone who creates the opening you have been searching for in your career. But you have to make it happen!

Your "one," your "Carson," could come in the form of a supervisor looking for the next great principal or access to the CEO who appreciates your unique skills. It could be the mentor who sees something in you that nobody else has seen. That "one" is out there. It's your job to position yourself so that they can find you. It may not happen overnight, but for everyone who has found success, that "one" pivotal person can change everything.

CARVE YOUR NICHE

I've documented how working in broadcasting differed from many of my peers. I was hit by several crushing layoffs, some of which nearly ended my career. Along the way, I encountered various obstacles, including naysayers and bad bosses, but I never lost sight of my pursuit of happiness. But eventually, I pivoted, using my core attributes to create new opportunities I had previously deemed impossible. The more chances I took, the more confident I became in my ability to trudge forward and succeed in those endeavors. If you told me in my 20s that in my 40s and 50s, I would create a segment called "Errands" for professional teams and own a production company servicing several nonprofits nationwide, I would have shaken my head.

The lesson: Pivoting creates happiness and opportunities you would never have known if you hadn't taken the chance!

Change is challenging, but the rewards are worth the effort for your career and your overall well-being. Pete Cataldo could have easily stayed a sportscaster or public relations professional, but he never would have found his happy place.

Pete found his true purpose by doing what many of you should and easily could do. He used his foundational skills to pivot towards success. We all have skills we take for granted. Don't waste them!

Today, Pete is in his 40s, and he's found the happiness he always sought in his career.

"I finally feel like I've done something that allows me to utilize my entire skillset," he said.

So, what advice would he give to other potential pivoters?

"If you've got an itch, there's a reason for it," he said. "Look into it. Pursue it."

There is no timetable for this. When you pivot, you work within your means.

"Never neglect the power of a side hustle," Pete attests. "That's what I did—racking up 10 years of coaching people before I started my own business. It doesn't have to be that long for you, or maybe it does need to be that long, or longer."

Patience is vital when pivoting. But the worst aspect of this mindset is regret. You don't want to look back at your life and wonder what you could have done to find happiness in your career.

"One thing I didn't want to happen was, I never wanted to look back and say to myself, 'What if?'" Pete said. "What if I didn't leave news? Would I be miserable? What if I didn't pursue my job in fitness? What if I did that? I don't want to hear that. Life is too short."

"If there is some sort of itch, something back there telling you it's worth it at least. Should I scratch it or ignore it?"

Gary Shandling made it to the top of his profession by pivoting and grinding, but he chose a unique path as he began to near the summit. Following his career-changing debut on "The Tonight Show," he was asked back and ultimately was given the platform to host the show occasionally. His reviews were so good in subsequent years that he was offered two great opportunities. One was the chance to replace David Letterman when Letterman left NBC. He turned that down. Later, he also turned

CBS down when they offered him a show that would follow Letterman.

Instead, he changed his career trajectory by making the ultimate late-night pivot. He did it by carving his niche and bypassing the traditional networks to create his own shows, first with "It's Gary Shandling's Show," and then with a sequel that proved legendary in the business, "The Larry Sanders Show." The latter wasn't a real talk show but a parody of all the behind-the-scenes drama of what went on in the late-night sphere.

In his story, "A Gary Shandling Photograph That Closes The Book On A Late-Night Era," Ian Crouch of The New Yorker wrote that after Shandling passed away, the comic's lasting legacy was the creation of the "Larry Sanders Show," a production that "punctured the cultural mythology of Late Night as well as reimagined what a sitcom might be." The article featured a picture of the Mt. Rushmore of Late Night hosts—Carson, Letterman, Leno, and Shandling. He never hosted a network show like the others, but his lasting legacy left him on the same plane.

The lesson: You chase what you love but create the most beneficial lane for your talents.

Shandling's pivot to the top of his profession was admirable. He built on his foundation and used all the steps I referenced in this book. He was able to conquer comedy, a notion that once scared him. He made the trip to see George Carlin and opened up a path to a writing career. He proved it was OK to quit writing as he had a distinct plan to pursue comedy.

His journey had Shandling discover Johnny Carson as the one who loved his work and set his career to a different level. He maximized relationships along the way to form his show and carve a niche for himself, which proved to be a career like no other comedic host has ever seen. Crouch wrote of Shandling's career, "Leno and Letterman were disciples of Carson, each in his way, then Shandling was more like a historian or critic, shading our memories and understanding of what we'd seen with commentary and metanarrative."

Pivoting from his foundation never ended for Shandling, who in his later years worked in different arenas, but it all surrounded his passion. He later moved from hosting to acting to voice-over work and ultimately became a mentor to many in his field.

"Comedy was always my underlying love," Shandling wrote in his documentary.

The lesson: Chase your dreams, but be aware of the power of sharing the knowledge you have gained to help others. Teaching and mentoring come in many different forms. Passing on your foundation is a powerful tool.

The great thing about doing what you love is sharing it. I became a college professor later in life, giving me a greater purpose than I could have imagined. It's nice to pass on the foundation of your craft while helping others overcome the many doubts you faced earlier in your career. This can take place in any walk of life and is something many take for granted. Teaching is a vehicle for this outlet, but it can take shape in many other forms. It doesn't necessarily mean teaching in a classroom. It can be in several areas, such as the workplace, an idle conversation, or a long phone call.

Many crave the information you've acquired and are eager to soak in your knowledge.

Passing on your foundation leaves others with the desired expertise you may take for granted but can inspire many. George Carlin probably never knew his brief critique of Shandling's work would make that seismic impact on his career, but it was tangible. A quality Shandling appreciated what he received and often paid it forward.

Shandling's willingness to share his foundation assisted many peers, including famed director Jon Favreau. Favreau, a respected actor, pivoted to directing and producing in his career and sought Shandling's advice for many of his Marvel blockbuster movies.

"The Iron Man (movie)," Favreau referenced in "The Zen Diaries of Gary Shandling," "had the kind of impact where I thought I had a special relationship with him because he was a bit of a mentor. There were dozens of people who felt this connection to the guy. The whole generation of people coming up and how generous he was with his time because I think he knew, especially the experience he had with George Carlin, a few words well placed can change the trajectory of somebody's career."

Inspiring others is one of many benefits of building from your foundation. It doesn't matter who you are. You have the passion and skills that come with it.

Finding your passion and pivoting from it are powerful tools that lead to endless possibilities.

So the choice is yours. The first step is usually the hardest, but once you take it, your confidence builds, and so do the results.

Make the most of what makes you great!

It's that simple. It begins and ends with your foundation, the gift that keeps giving. It's your choice—to use the gifts you've been given and do what you love the most.

And remember ... it's never too late to get going!

CHAPTER NINE

FINDING YOUR HAPPY "BEGINNING"

"When you think you are at the end of something, you are the beginning of something else."
Fred Rogers

This book has referenced pivoters from every direction: actors, musicians, bodybuilders, wrestlers, and even skateboarders.

The goal is to pass on the idea that the ability to move from one career to something better for you is attainable for everyone.

When thinking about pivoting, always know that you're not alone. Several others have blazed the trail in various ways and a plethora of careers.

The examples are endless, touching every occupation and potential hobby.

PIVOTING TO A GREAT CAUSE

Entrepreneur Zach Wigal's passion was video games. In 2008, he founded the nonprofit Gamers Outreach, which provides gaming experiences to children in hospitals worldwide. It was an unlikely pivot for Wigal, who started this charity after hosting a high school video game tournament that raised money for a local charity.

Wigal's pivot was born from the realization that there was a demand for entertainment for young patients unable to leave their hospital beds, so he brought gaming to them. Wigal purchased the games via a portable, medical-grade video game kiosk called GO Kart. He told the gaming website Game Rant, "We want video games to be fully integrated with health care facilities."

This innovative effort affects millions. Wigal's nonprofit, "Gamers Outreach," has touched over 400 hospitals, providing more than 4.3 million gaming experiences annually.

PIVOTING IN A WHOLE NEW DIRECTION

This book has highlighted some versatile pivots, including Schwarzenegger's transformation from bodybuilder to actor to governor. However, Ingrid Nilsen boasts quite the innovative career jump.

This modern-day pivoter was a successful YouTube creator with 3.46 million subscribers, but had lost her zest for keeping that career going. Nilsen had many creative interests, including candle making, which she had picked up during the pandemic. What started as a hobby quickly became a full-time endeavor, and for Nilsen, making the pivot from online creator to candlestick maker brought more passion and happiness.

Alongside partner Erica Andersen, Nilsen co-founded The New Savant, a Brooklyn-based scent studio that brought customers a unique perspective. The studio featured a variety of creative candles inspired by Nilsen's life. For example, "Mixed Feelings" is a candle influenced by Nilsen's mixed heritage, while "Library in a Forest" represents her love of nature, books, and fantasy.

Her creative niche has paved the way for a successful pivot, which has equated to a new career and newfound happiness. "I love that I'm always doing something different," Nilsen tells Eater.com's Morgan Goldberg.

"Some days, I'm focused heavily on creating new fragrances. Other days I'm testing samples from our perfumers or working on marketing campaigns and new launches. Sometimes it's working with the art department for product photo shoots. We do everything in-house. But I'd say my favorite part is when I get to be hands-on with my team in the studio. I love the basics of making candles, so when I get to pour, label, or pack up orders with the team, it feels like reconnecting with my roots."

Clearly, the passion is there for Nilsen, who was asked by Goldberg,

"What's the best piece of career advice you've been given?" Nilsen passed on a line she heard from an inspiring TED Talk, "I didn't need my dream to be easy, I just needed it to be possible."

A PAINTING PIVOT

While Nilsen and Wigal aren't household names, actress Sharon Stone has been one for over three decades. The versatile actor has starred in box office smashes such as "Basic Instinct," "Casino" and "Total Recall," but you may wonder why you don't see her in as many movies anymore? The answer falls in line with this book.

She pivoted.

Stone hasn't given up acting, but her pivot was toward her first love, painting. Her aunt taught her the craft as a young girl in rural Pennsylvania. Stone didn't let go of that passion growing up, and her work was such that she could sell paintings to get by in college.

Acting would take over her life for decades, but during COVID-19, a friend gave Stone a paint-by-numbers kit, which rekindled her love and set the stage for a career pivot. Her paintings would attract gallery shows coast to coast, from Los Angeles to Greenwich, Connecticut, and eventually international audiences.

For years, everyone around Stone tended to limit her options, "Everybody told me to stay in my lane and my lane started to get narrow," she told CBS "This Morning's" Lee Cowan in 2024. But Stone sees painting as an extension of her acting talents. "I don't think I'm just an actress or a writer or a painter, I think I'm an artist."

Her painting prowess typifies everything this book wants to convey about pivoting. When Stone talks about how she approaches each of her projects, it symbolizes our fear when we are confronted with the possibility of making a change in our lives.

"I think if you listen to the highest consciousness and follow that voice," Stone told CBS, "How do you go wrong with that? I'm letting it start to evolve and tell me what it wants to be."

So, we can use Stone's approach to painting as a metaphor for all of us who listen deep inside to our inner voice telling us to follow our hearts and our passions.

Trusting our instincts has paid off for many "pivoters," including Stone, who is happier at this stage in her life with a paintbrush than with a leading role on the big screen.

"I do it because I'm fully and wholly immersed in it, and I love it. I'd rather do it (painting) than anything else."

I didn't want to write this book until I did it, too.

I had to pivot.

Trust me, I talked about it and thought about it for years, but there was a wake-up call that pushed me past all of my fear, procrastination, and self-doubt. What was my pivotal point?

I turned 50.

At that moment, I thought, 'Stop talking and start doing. Stop worrying about your current career and do everything you thought you could.'

It was time to take action.

My 50th awakening saw me pivot to a new life on many fronts.

I knew I wanted to teach, so I returned to school for my master's degree. My goal was to get a job as a college professor teaching broadcasting in a communication school.

That's when another pivot happened.

A friend heard I wanted to teach and introduced me to the dean of a business school. He hired me on the spot to teach a class he titled "Sports Innovation and Entrepreneurship."

The dean told me, here's the title. You run with it.

Let the pivoting begin.

I remember walking into that first class. It was a night course and longer than most courses; it was designated for three hours. This was quite the hurdle for a rookie professor who wasn't sure if this pivot was going to work.

What did I do?

Over the next few weeks and years, I leaned on my many decades of work experience. I trusted my instincts and used the skills I had acquired over the past 35 years as a broadcast journalist and entrepreneur to guide me.

At first, it wasn't easy, but I was motivated. This new profession had the potential to make me the happiest I've ever been, and it has. My years of experience in television production and writing helped me create lectures that got easier over time.

My penchant for creativity enabled me to devise fun class exercises for my students. My contacts brought me guest speakers from every angle—sports marketing, management, and media.

My entrepreneurial background helped me complement what I was teaching with real-world thinking and a perspective on what has worked and what hasn't. My students seemed to appreciate hearing this.

After two years as a full-time instructor, I was voted "Professor of the Year" at my business school. I'm not passing this on to flaunt an award; moreover, to prove that while I had never taken a marketing, management, or entrepreneurship course in my life, my experiences and skills over many decades enabled me to pivot to untapped success in a career I had never dreamed would bring such happiness.

The same can happen to you!

We all have skills we take for granted. Until I started teaching, I thought maybe the traits I picked up in years of television were only good for media jobs. No, our skills can help us in many different careers. We need to test the boundaries.

In Marshall Goldsmith's New York Times bestselling book, "The Earned Life," he writes about his friend Sanyin Siang, the co-founder and director of the Coach K Center on Leadership & Ethics at Duke University. The center, named after legendary Duke basketball coach Mike Krzyzewski, believes "each of us has at least one skill that we take for granted and are perplexed when we discover that it's out of reach for everyone else."

Siang calls this "the liability of expertise," which could include those who can throw a baseball at 100 mph or juggle with ease. We all need to use the skills we acquire. According to Goldsmith, Siang says, "It's like having a superpower and not using it."

Find your superpower ... and use it!

In Arthur C. Brooks's book, "Strength to Strength," Brooks recognizes that we all have strengths, but how do we use them? "We are all born with gifts," Brooks writes. "No matter how you find your passion early on, pursue it with a white-hot flame, dedicating it to the good of the world."

Brooks highlights that we all have the potential to contribute great things, but we need to recognize that a pivot is often required for all of us to reach our collective potential. "But hold your success lightly-be ready to change as your abilities change. Remember, every change of circumstance is a chance to learn, grow and create value."

Prepare to pivot!

You can't put a price on the potential rewards for using your abilities to the fullest. "We are living an earned life when the choices, risks, and effort we make in each moment align with an overarching purpose in our lives, regardless of the eventual outcome," Goldsmith highlights in his book, "The Earned Life."

Using your skills to find your passion is vital, but as I mentioned at the book's onset, often the hardest part is getting started. Whatever goals we strive for, deviating from our desired path isn't easy. It's common to find endless excuses for why you can't make the bold move or exert the effort to make your pivot happen.

Goldsmith focuses on the many excuses for staying on the sidelines in favor of getting into the game or, for our purposes, your desired pivot.
- **The Indispensability Argument** states that you lean on the premise that your organization needs you, which keeps you from moving forward or following your desired passion.
- **The Winner's Argument**—the notion that whomever you're working for, "we're on a hot streak. It's too soon to quit." Sometimes, it's easier to stay in a successful situation even when it's not making you happy.
- **The No-Place-To-Go-Argument**: this applies to those who are lost. You have the mindset of "I have no idea what I want to do next."

As I noted in this book, fear is often our primary motivator for moving past the excuses and making it happen. Doing something you're scared of provides you with the pivot you need and the confidence that fuels your future success.

Fear is present for everyone, from CEOs to college students. Brooks' "Strength to Strength" surveys both arenas, where researchers have discovered that public speaking is the most common fear among college students. Scholars have famously asserted that people fear it more than death.

As a professor, I acknowledge this and remember how petrified I was to stand up before my peers when I was my students' age. So, I try to mitigate this with my students on the first day. I have them stand up on day one and twice a week for the rest of the semester. It was uncomfortable initially for many, but several have communicated to me that constantly fighting the fear each week made them better.

While students fear speaking, CEOs fear failure. According to a 2018 survey from Norwest Venture Partners, an American venture and growth equity investment firm, "90% of CEOs admit fear of failure keeps them up at night more than any other concern."

I have covered sports for decades and know the best coaches concur with that notion. For years, when I covered Bobby Bowden, he consistently stated that fear was his constant motivator. The fear of losing consumed him even at the peak of his success at Florida State. "It's a feeling that I betrayed everybody, that nobody likes me anymore. It's an inferiority problem like people are ashamed of me."

Fighting fear and excuses is often accomplished by establishing a new routine and habits, which empower all of us to focus better on the bigger goals. In James Clear's New York Times bestselling book, "Atomic Habits," he provides "an operating manual" that serves as a step-by-step action plan for building better habits. Many of the book's tenets are invaluable for those looking to pivot towards their respective happy *beginnings*.

Clear's theme steers you from setting goals, which he feels restricts happiness. The key to establishing a quality routine is finding something you love. "When you fall in love with the process rather than the product, you don't have to wait to give yourself permission to be happy. You can be satisfied anytime your system is running."

This mindset from Clear emphasizes the interesting notion that "the purpose of setting goals is to win the game. The purpose of building systems is to continue playing the game."

We want to pivot to a passion that has staying power! To accomplish this, you must fall in love with your craft, and that means falling in love with your routine.

Allow your routine to become your passion. Clear writes, "It's one thing to say I'm the type of person who wants this. It's something very different to say I'm the type of person who is this."

Actor Ethan Hawke fell in love with his craft out of necessity. "My Mom wanted me to get busy," he told Time magazine. Hawke's form of busy was joining a local theatre at a young age, where he quickly deciphered two early impressions—this new environment was fun, and the people around him, including the grown-ups, were enjoying their work.

This was a stark contrast to what he was used to at home.

"My parents hated their jobs; they were working on the weekends. The jobs were something to be gotten through so you could do something else."

Hawke knew he didn't want to adopt this mindset where acting provided an early avenue to fall in love with a career with seemingly endless possibilities.

"I just want to do this, the rest of my life."

It's one thing to realize where your passion lies; it's yet another to understand that you often won't master it overnight. For Hawke, acting took time to master.

This is a valuable lesson in pivoting. Passion will get you through the hard times, but you need to realize that they will happen. You must ask yourself, do you love what you do enough to want to get better?

"Well you're gonna suck at it," Hawk confessed about acting at first. "Don't worry about that. You gotta suck at it. There's no way to be good at anything without sucking."

"You just gotta put in the practice and the humility to say, 'I'm not great.'"

So we've addressed facing your fears and knowing you have to put the work in, but for many, it's still a matter of falling in love with something enough to make that pivot. We solve this natural progression by weighing the skills we've acquired over the years to see if creating these new options is viable.

Learning so much after decades of being a sportscaster and entrepreneur propelled me to become a college professor, author, and speaker.

After finding early success, Ethan Hawke took some money from his first big hit, "Dead Poet's Society," and pivoted to a new role at the young age of 21, where he "directed" his first short film.

Hawke was passionate about acting but knew early on that being in front of the camera wouldn't be his sole option. "It seemed awfully arrogant that I could keep acting my whole life. I felt like I needed to learn to write and direct to make sure I still had a job when I was 50."

Many (including me) feel they are meant to do one thing in life. Often, though, we need to pivot. It's scary, and it takes discipline, but the rewards are endless. Ask Hawke, who has found that directing has opened more doors and provided much more happiness.

"If you want to know who you are, the easiest definition for it, you know what you do love," Hawke told Time. "If you really think about what you love and you get close to it, then your love starts to expand, and you start to know yourself."

The beauty of pivoting is that it's never too late to fall in love with your next passion.

In her book, "Reinventing You," author Dorie Clark found that chasing your dreams has no expiration date.

"There was a guy I knew whose father had gone back to graduate school in his sixties and got his PhD at age 68."

"A lot of people would say a PhD program that's five years, seven years, eight years. You're in your 60s, why would you do that? Why would you bother? Shouldn't you be retiring?"

"But this was a person who had a lifelong love of learning. He thought it would be an interesting intellectual quest. He didn't know where it was going to lead, but he was excited to see, and I think that's an attitude that more of us need to have."

"The way that we talk about the world of work has really not caught up to the fact that people are commonly living into their 90s now. Like, somehow, we imagined that you turn 70ish and you drop off a cliff, and for the vast majority of people who are from a reasonably affluent background and have access to healthcare, that is no longer the case. You can safely assume statistically that you will be living into your mid-80s and beyond," Clark told me.

"So the idea that somehow we should give up on our professional aspirations when we hit 50 is extremely out of date. I mean, sure, if you want to make a conscious decision and you have enough money and you want to golf forever, that's amazing."

50 was a wake-up call for me, but that wake-up call can happen at several advanced ages. Don't let age define when you pivot and what your impact can be.

Some of the most successful people started their careers late in life.

After being an engineer for Thomas Edison for years, Henry Ford graduated to become a successful machinist and car designer. Still, it wasn't until he was 40 that Ford founded the Ford Motor Company. This late bloomer would pivot to create the Model T at 45 and institute the assembly line, which became a standard for the car industry.

Famed American chef, author, and TV personality Julia Child never learned how to cook until she met her husband in her thirties. She pivoted to her cooking fame after serving as a clerk for a United States Intelligence agency in World War II.

One of the biggest success stories at an advanced age was Harland David Sanders, who eventually gained fame and wealth as Colonel Sanders. Growing up in a poor family, Sanders learned to cook when he was seven. Before pivoting to a restaurant owner, he would have many jobs, including steam engine stoker, insurance salesman, and filling station operator.

Sanders started selling his secret fried chicken recipe during the Great Depression. He then founded a series of small restaurants inside gas stations until, at the advanced age of 62, he launched his first Kentucky Fried

Chicken franchise. It became a fast food powerhouse. Sanders sold his franchises in 1964 for 2 million, but it's worth nearly 20 million today.

Pivoting doesn't discriminate when it comes to age!

"Devote the back half of your life to serving others with your wisdom. Get old sharing the things you believe are most important. Excellence is always its own reward, and this is how you can be most excellent at your age," Arthur Brooks writes in "From Strength to Strength."

It doesn't matter if you're Ethan Hawke, who fell in love with acting as a child, or Sharon Stone, who fell in love with painting in her mid-60s. The power of pivoting hits us at all ages. It's liberating and life changing.

Brooks writes, "Your biggest life transition doesn't have to be a crisis or a period of loss but rather can be an exciting adventure full of opportunities you never knew existed."

That's the exciting part—the unknown. If someone had told me when I was 40 that I would be teaching, writing books, and speaking in my 50s, I would have shaken my head, but it's the happiest I've ever been.

Making a monumental pivot in your life comes down to really examining your approach to your career and how you can improve where ultimately you will find happiness you couldn't have possibly imagined.

"The tighter we cling to an identity, the harder it becomes to grow beyond it," Clear writes in "Atomic Habits." "The more you let a single belief define you, the less capable you are of adapting when life challenges you."

It's easier to face life's challenges when you are happy doing what you love. But to find happiness, we must be self-aware and realize what changes we must undertake to open new doors for our dreams.

Clear emphasizes, "Life is constantly changing, so you need to periodically check in to see if your old habits and beliefs are still serving you. A lack of self-awareness is poison. Reflection and review are the antidotes."

Clear's four laws of behavior change are the following:
- Make it Obvious
- Make it Attractive
- Make it Easy
- Make it Satisfying

When you love something, all of the above are easier to attain.

Pivoting can help you find your happy "beginning," too!

REACHING YOUR FINISH LINE

Ultimately, creating your happiness will give you many things. It will grant you a liberating feeling you have always dreamed about. However, putting yourself out there and making the pivot you've been striving for is a feeling you will likely not want to experience just once. Frankly, you will enjoy it so much that you want to experience it repeatedly.

Pivoting can be contagious! Once you climb one mountain, it will provide the confidence to do so much more.

This book has chronicled several examples, from Arnold Schwarzenegger to Dick Vitale to Lisa Kudrow and Michael Strahan—bold people who trusted their instincts and pivoted towards greater happiness. We've followed the zigs and zags of several pivotal journeys of entrepreneurs and dream chasers who knew there was something better in their journeys and dared to bet on themselves.

Changing the course of your life isn't easy, but the rewards are indescribable.

At the beginning of the book, I mentioned how the most challenging part is often getting out of the starting gate—putting yourself out there, whether it's making that first phone call, scheduling that initial meeting, or, in my case, writing the first paragraph of this book.

Whatever the process, at some point, the light will go on that you are moving in the right direction. You experience progress and development, which fosters confidence. When you finally see your finish line, it's frankly a feeling like no other.

Understand that it's human to feel that day will never come. You must trust the process. Keep in mind that if it was easy, as my Dad would say, "everybody would do it." Finding your finish line will be so much more valuable if it's hard and you survive all the ups and downs of your respective pivots.

I can't tell you how rewarding the finish lines have been since I turned 50. Getting my thesis approved and receiving my master's degree, finishing my first semester of teaching, speaking at my first event, and writing the last words of my latest book—it's a satisfying feeling on so many levels.

Hopefully, this book will encourage you to take that first step and find your finish line one day. Do something that scares you, broaden your network and maximize your relationships, make your trip, whatever that may be, and realize it often only takes one person to help jumpstart your new avenue of happiness.

If you are willing, the exciting challenges await you, enabling you to enjoy all of the possibilities you never thought were possible.

Now, seize the opportunity and go for it!

ACKNOWLEDGMENTS

I want to thank the many who helped make this project happen. My editor, good friend, and veteran writer, Roy Cummings, for shaping this book the way I wanted with all its moving parts. Thanks to the legendary Dick Vitale for his constant support over the years, from being the "godfather" of "Errands" to writing the Foreword. "Dickie V"—you are one of one, my friend! A big thanks to Amy Cianci and the team at St. Petersburg Press for navigating this book "every" step of the way. A sincere salute to my peers Pat Clarke, Jason Alpert, Pete Cataldo, and Drew Fellios for their extended Zoom interviews, which provided needed perspective for this book. I appreciate the time of respected author and professor Dorie Clark for delivering exceptional insight to complement the fundamental tenets of this project. I appreciate the perspectives of respected authors Marshall Goldsmith, Wayne Baker, Arthur C. Brooks, Malcolm Gladwell, and James Clear, who motivated me to write about a topic that aims to help many find happiness. Finally, thanks to many whose names aren't listed in this book but are referenced (you know who you are), who have taught me so much and pushed me to the finish line. I appreciate you all!

WORKS CITED

Dan Patrick Show. "Darius Rucker on the Dan Patrick Show Full Interview | 08/12/22." *YouTube*, 12 Aug. 2022, youtu.be/VgjlH3uX81o?si=d-Q_42DFzf4JyKFQ9. Accessed 13 June 2024.

Pajer, Nicole. "Jennifer Grey Is out of the Corner! The Dirty Dancing Star Talks Self-Worth, Plastic Surgery and Mental Wellness." *Parade*, 8 May 2022, parade.com/1378344/nicolepajer/jennifer-grey-mental-health/.

The Rich Eisen Show. ""Just Getting Started" with Rich Eisen - Voices of the NFL: Michael Strahan." *YouTube*, 2 Oct. 2021, youtu.be/MIKNaOoOOUE?si=ErTvFbJJsUgoga1M. Accessed 13 June 2024.

Clark, Dorie, and Natalie Nixon. "The Challenge of Leaving a Long-Term Job to Start Something New." *Harvard Business Review*, 6 May 2024, hbr.org/2024/05/the-challenge-of-leaving-a-long-term-job-to-start-something-new. Accessed 9 July 2024.

Clark, Dorie. *Reinventing You, with a New Preface*. Harvard Business Press, 12 Sept. 2017.

AXS TV. "How Darius Rucker Fell in Love with Country Music | the Big Interview." *YouTube*, 20 May 2024, youtu.be/8Yf_prFqBrE?si=FVo5Vo3x-TPKwgy2. Accessed 13 June 2024.

TODAY. "Darius Rucker Talks New Music, Mother's Support and David Letterman Boost." *YouTube*, 8 Oct. 2023, youtu.be/6w44aQ0h-cO8?si=9eWaqDf_cgFMydpW. Accessed 13 June 2024.

Vassar. "Lisa Kudrow Commencement Address 2010." *YouTube*, 4 June 2010, youtu.be/uLkUoeMNeeY?si=X9kZMuETKCNYmrad. Accessed

13 June 2024.

The Kelly Clarkson Show. "Lisa Kudrow Wanted to Be a Doctor before Acting." *YouTube*, 15 July 2022, youtu.be/QAxfvYfSFqY?si=Zgq7b-2JqCOBhyf8G. Accessed 13 June 2024.

Grohl, David. *The Storyteller : Tales of Life and Music*. New York, Ny, Dey St., An Imprint Of William Morrow, 2021.

Netflix. "Arnold | Netflix." *YouTube*, 10 May 2023, youtu.be/x2AEI26LBpA?si=eNfc-RzR0ed6BFl2.

Buckingham, M., 2022. Designing work that people love. *Harvard Business Review, 100*(5-6), pp.66-75.

Chamorro-Premuzic, Tomas. *Why Do so Many Incompetent Men Become Leaders?* Harvard Business Press, 19 Feb. 2019.

The Howard Stern Show. "Why Molly Shannon Left "Saturday Night Live."" *YouTube*, 12 Apr. 2022, youtu.be/Y1vF6HQCyj0?si=QY7U8uZ-FIxGUaimD. Accessed 8 July 2024.

HBO. "Tony Hawk: Until the Wheels Fall off | Official Trailer | HBO." *YouTube*, 8 Mar. 2022, youtu.be/iqhmW_etP38?si=m2qEqonQ8i9Ttx9f. Accessed 8 July 2024.

Duncan, Rodger Dean. "Need Help? Don't Be Afraid to Ask." *Forbes*, 1 Sept. 2020, www.forbes.com/sites/rodgerdeanduncan/2020/09/01/need-help-dont-be-afraid-to-ask/#:~:text=Defying%20the%20age%2Dold%20adage. Accessed 8 July 2024.

Baker, Wayne E. *All You Have to Do Is Ask : How to Master the Most Important Skill for Success*. New York, Currency, 2020.

Brooks, A.W., F. Gino, and M.E. Schweitzer. "Smart People Ask for (My) Advice: Seeking Advice Boosts Perceptions of Competence." Management Science 61, no. 6 (June 2015): 1421–1435.

Sam Farmer. "Peyton Manning Is a True Man of Letters, the Handwritten Kind." *Los Angeles Times*, 28 May 2013, www.latimes.com/sports/

la-xpm-2013-may-28-la-sp-peyton-manning-letters-20130528-story.html. Accessed 8 July 2024.

Benbow, Dana Hunsinger. "Peyton Manning Is Making Cold Calls to Indy Liquor Stores to Put His Bourbon on Shelves." *The Indianapolis Star*, 22 Sept. 2021, www.indystar.com/story/sports/nfl/colts/2021/09/22/peyton-manning-calls-indy-liquor-stores-his-bourbon/5754887001/. Accessed 8 July 2024.

The Pivot Podcast. "The Rock: Vulnerabilities, Being a Girl Dad, Future of XFL & How Wrestling Saved My Life | the Pivot." *YouTube*, 9 May 2023, youtu.be/MVc0592Je_o?si=SZt_MH1ubU-otaiY. Accessed 8 July 2024.

Smith, Morgan. "Black Women Are the Fastest-Growing Group of Entrepreneurs in the U.S.—Meet 3 Who Grew Their Side Hustles into Successful Businesses." *CNBC*, 18 Feb. 2024, www.cnbc.com/2024/02/18/black-women-are-the-fastest-growing-group-of-entrepreneurs-in-the-us.html.

HBO. "George Carlin's American Dream | Official Trailer | HBO." *YouTube*, 2 May 2022, youtu.be/TWCGCacySrQ?si=RZcNN-hLDlHeY-ROB. Accessed 8 July 2024.

SmartLess. "11/1/21: An Interview with Jerry Seinfeld | SmartLess W/ Jason Bateman, Sean Hayes, Will Arnett." *YouTube*, 3 Nov. 2021, youtu.be/VcXWQsEaaXE?si=UPIEz2yBcbjlUZlY.

Steinberg, David. *Inside Comedy*. University Press of Kentucky, 13 July 2021.

Remnick, David. "The Scholar of Comedy." *The New Yorker*, 28 Apr. 2024, www.newyorker.com/culture/the-new-yorker-interview/the-scholar-of-comedy.

Writer, Zach Schonfeld Senior. "Q&A: Steve Martin on Bluegrass, Why He Ditched Movies." *Newsweek*, 12 Sept. 2017, www.newsweek.com/steve-martin-movies-banjo-steep-canyon-rangers-663523.

Wylie, PL. "Garry Shandling." *Www.entertaintucson.com*, 1 Jan. 1986, www.entertaintucson.com/volumeone/garryshandling.html.

"The Zen Diaries of Garry Shandling (2018)| HBO." *YouTube*, 22 Feb. 2018, youtu.be/paerP97n4aA?si=LicCL1ncad5mm1bZ.

Crouch, Ian. "A Garry Shandling Photograph That Closes the Book on a Late-Night Era." *The New Yorker*, 28 Mar. 2016, www.newyorker.com/culture/cultural-comment/a-garry-shandling-photograph-that-closes-the-book-on-a-late-night-era. Accessed 9 July 2024.

Johnson, Gemma. "Gamers Outreach Founder Zach Wigal Discusses Bringing People Together, Supporting Patients, and More." *Game Rant*, 28 Feb. 2023, gamerant.com/gamers-outreach-interview-charity-hospitals/.

Goldberg, Morgan. "How I Got My Job: Making Internet-Famous Food-Inspired Candles." *Eater*, 12 Jan. 2024, www.eater.com/24031674/how-to-become-candlemaker-ingrid-nilson-the-new-savant-interview-food-scent-candles.

CBS Sunday Morning. "Sharon Stone, Artist." *YouTube*, 21 Jan. 2024, youtu.be/qWlUeAy8LMU?si=XrL4s7XW6mITg5GQ. Accessed 9 July 2024.

Goldsmith, Marshall, and Mark Reiter. *The Earned Life*. Currency, 3 May 2022.

Brooks, Arthur C. *From Strength to Strength*. Penguin, 15 Feb. 2022.

Kahneman, Daniel, Krueger. Alan B, Schkade, David A, et al (2004). "A Survey Method for Characterizing Daily Life Experience: The Day Reconstruction Method" Science, (306) (5702), 1776-80.

"Findings from Our CEO Journey Study." *Norwest Venture Partners*, www.nvp.com/blog/insights-norwests-2018-ceo-journey-study/. Accessed 16 July 2024.

Clear, James. *Atomic Habits: An Easy and Proven Way to Build Good Habits and Break Bad Ones*. Penguin Random House, 2018.

www.ingramcontent.com/pod-product-compliance
Lightning Source LLC
Chambersburg PA
CBHW050243010526
44107CB00032B/1387/J